Handbook of Basic Citizenship Competencies

Guidelines for Comparing Materials,
Assessing Instruction and Setting Goals

Richard C. Remy

Association for Supervision and Curriculum Development

225 North Washington Street, Alexandria, Virginia 22314

Stock number: 611-80196
Library of Congress Catalog Card Number: 79-56888
ISBN: 0-87120-098-8

The National
Institute of
Education
U.S. Department of
Health, Education and Welfare
Washington, D.C. 20208

This publication was prepared with funding from the National Institute of Education, U.S. Department of Health, Education and Welfare under contract no. 400-78-0050. The opinions expressed in this report do not necessarily reflect the positions or policies of NIE or HEW.

Acknowledgments

The Basic Citizenship Competencies Project wishes to acknowledge the contribution of the following individuals who served as members of the National Advisory Panel for this project.

Dr. Charlotte Anderson
Assistant Director
Law & Humanities Project
American Bar Association

Dr. Lee Anderson
Professor of Political Science
  and Education
Northwestern University

Mr. Urban J. Bear Don't Walk
Attorney-at-Law
Billings, Montana

Dr. Kenneth Benne
Professor Emeritus
Philosophy & Organizational
  Development
Boston University

Dr. Donald H. Bragaw
Chief, Instructional Services
The State Department of Education
The University of the State of
  New York

Ms. Carolyn Burkhardt
Program Associate
National Center for Research in
  Vocational Education

Dr. Janet Eyler
Social Studies Education
George Peabody College

Dr. Carole Hahn
School of Education
Emory University

Ms. Edna Jean Harper
Teacher
Columbus Public Schools

Mrs. Carol Kimmel
Immediate Past President
National Parent Teachers Assn.
Rock Island, Illinois

Dr. Roger LaRaus
School District #65
Evanston, Illinois

Mrs. Eva Legarde
Chairperson, ESEA
Advisory Panel for Title I
East Baton Rouge Parish
Baton Rouge, Louisiana

Dr. Evelyn Luckey
Assistant Superintendent
Columbus, Ohio Public Schools

Ms. Charen Martinez
Teacher, Junior High Social Studies
Westminster, Colorado

Dr. John Patrick
Professor of Education
Indiana University

Mr. Martin Shallenberger
Senior Staff P.A. Representative
Standard Oil Company (Ind.)

Dr. Roberta Sigel
Department of Political Science
Rutgers University

Dr. Barbara Winston
Associate Professor
Northeastern Illinois University

The American Political Science
Association's Committee on Pre-
Collegiate Education

Professor L. Harmon Zeigler
Center for Educational Policy &
  Management
University of Oregon

School Principals Group

Ms. Catherine Crandell
Valleyview Elementary,
  Columbus, Ohio

Mr. Titus A. Saunders, Jr.
Mohawk Junior High School,
  Columbus, Ohio

Mr. Roger Dumaree
Columbus South High School,
  Columbus, Ohio

Mr. Ronald G. Sroufe
Whetstone High School,
  Columbus, Ohio

Ms. Catherine M. Feike
Douglas Alternative School,
  Columbus, Ohio

Mr. Curtis A. Smith
Bexley Junior High School,
  Bexley, Ohio

Contents

Basic Citizenship Competencies Project

This publication was prepared as part of the Basic Citizenship Competencies Project. The project is a joint undertaking of the Mershon Center, The Ohio State University and the Social Science Education Consortium (SSEC), Boulder, Colorado, with support from the National Institute of Education. Richard C. Remy (Mershon Center) and Mary Jane Turner (SSEC) are the project codirectors. The project has been assisted by a national advisory panel consisting of 25 political scientists, educators and citizens, as well as the American Political Science Association's Committee on Precollegiate Education.

During 1978-79 the project examined research, theory and practice related to political behavior and learning in order to establish conceptual definitions, develop a typology of basic citizenship competencies and prepare written materials for practitioners. The goal of these activities was to use existing knowledge to create problem-solving tools that could assist practitioners to identify basics, clarify goals, make assessments and develop action plans related to citizen education.

In addition to this handbook, written materials developed by the project include a leadership guide for principals and checklists for teachers, parents and community leaders. Contact the Basic Citizenship Competencies Project, Mershon Center, 199 West 10th Avenue, Columbus, Ohio 43201 for information on these materials.

About the Author

Richard C. Remy is an associate professor at The Ohio State University, where he holds appointments in the Political Science and Humanities Education departments. Dr. Remy is also director of the Citizenship Development Program at Ohio State University's Mershon Center. He began his career as a classroom teacher in the Chicago Public Schools. His articles on political science, curriculum and instruction have appeared in many professional journals. He has written extensively for young students on citizenship and decision making. He has also served as a consultant to numerous school systems and state departments of education.

Foreword

Preparing young people to be the responsible citizens of tomorrow has long been a major goal of education. Traditionally, schools have readied students for citizenship by teaching government and history and by emphasizing such activities as saluting the flag, participating in student government, and occasional involvement in the political elective process.

Yet today's youth face a complex and confusing world of big government and convoluted international relations. Technological innovations have accelerated changes in values and institutions. The Vietnam War and Watergate have created mistrust of government; the energy crisis has forced Americans to reevaluate conventional attitudes and practices.

How do we equip this generation of young people to participate effectively in civic and public life? How do we teach them to communicate well with others, make competent decisions, and promote and protect their interests as members of groups in responsible ways? What activities will help youngsters appreciate the responsibilities and rewards of citizenship?

The purpose of this booklet is to spell out clearly the skills needed by citizens so that we will be in a better position to design educational programs for developing these skills. Research and theory have indicated seven basic competencies which individuals need to exercise responsibilities effectively and protect their interests as citizens. These are: 1. Acquiring and using information; 2. Assessing involvement; 3. Making decisions; 4. Making judgments; 5. Communicating; 6. Cooperating; 7. Promoting interests.

This booklet covers each of these interrelated areas in detail. Suggested classroom activities for various age levels are included. Also provided are criteria for evaluating citizenship-related learning experiences, a helpful "citizenship for educators."

Educating effective citizens is one of the most important challenges our society faces. Yet there is evidence that some of the youth in America are lacking in basic political knowledge, skills, and attitudes. The importance of a book to aid administrators and teachers in evaluating citizenship educational policies and programs cannot be overemphasized. We are grateful to the Mershon Foundation and the Citizenship Competencies Project for making it possible for ASCD to publish the results of their work in this area.

Benjamin P. Ebersole
President, ASCD, 1979-80

Preface

A major educational aim in the future is to develop a citizenry that is politically, economically and scientifically literate.—Ralph Tyler

What constitutes basic education in citizenship for today's students? What competencies must students develop if they are to discharge their responsibilities and protect their interests as citizens? How can we identify instructional materials and school management practices likely to promote basic citizenship competencies?

This handbook is designed to assist teachers, supervisors and curriculum specialists as they develop, implement and assess programs relevant to education for citizenship. The handbook provides an introduction and guide to basic elements of citizenship education today.

Originally, in the public school concept, citizenship education was a major focus of all education. To some extent this is still the case. However, since the 1920s citizenship education also has been treated as a special concern of the social studies area of the curriculum. Further, research indicates that the social organization of schools and the classroom makes up an "informal" citizenship curriculum that affects political learning in important but not yet fully understood ways.

This handbook has six chapters. Chapter 1 introduces the purpose of the handbook. Chapter 2 identifies seven basic citizenship competencies. The third chapter describes these competencies and related capacities in detail. Examples of learning experiences for each competency are also presented. Chapter 4 provides criteria for evaluating citizenship-related learning experiences. Chapter 5 presents instructions for using a checklist as a diagnostic tool for comparing instructional materials; assessing goals, objectives and classroom instruction, and setting new goals related to citizenship education. The sixth chapter considers the meaning of citizenship. Notes and a bibliography are also provided. The Appendix contains the complete Citizenship Competency Checklist for teachers' use and a special checklist for parents.

1. Introduction

Horace Mann was referring to citizenship education when he observed:

> In order that men may be prepared for self-government, their apprenticeship must commence in childhood. The great moral attribute of self-government cannot be born and matured in a day; and if school children are not trained to it, we only prepare ourselves for disappointment.[1]

Citizenship education involves learning and instruction related to the development of citizen competence. Learning may be seen as "a relatively permanent change in competence that results from experience and which is not attributable to physical maturation."[2] Instruction involves structuring a learner's environment to cause changes in capability. It is "the creation of conditions that facilitate learning."[3] Citizenship education can occur both in school and in nonschool settings. The development of competent citizens is the overall goal of citizenship education.

Some political scientists call this process *political education*.[4] One recently described the process as involving "the training of people in the knowledge, skills and attitudes which are prerequisite for active and effective participation in civic life." The goal of this process, she added, "should be mature citizens who can both advocate and carry out appropriate political actions to further their perceived self-interest, while evaluating longer-range perspective[s] . . . within some framework of the 'common good.'"[5] In this sense, citizenship education is a continuing challenge for each succeeding generation. As societal conditions change, various facets of citizenship education will also change. However, the basic challenge of equipping people to behave competently in an imperfect world will remain.

Three conditions make it useful to systematically consider what constitute basic elements of citizenship education for today's students. First, citizenship has become more complex in the sense that the number and complexity of tasks and responsibilities associated with the citizen role has greatly increased. Critical societal changes in recent decades affecting citizenship have included the rise of global interdependence; the growth of large-scale institutions, especially big government; technological innovation and a knowledge explosion; the reemergence of racial and ethnic consciousness; the growth of concern for equality of opportunity; and an increase in alienation from social institutions, including public schools and large government.

Second, as our society has become more complex, citizenship education has become increasingly diversified. Citizenship education in the school today, for example, may include not only the familiar civics, history, and geography, but also such topics as law-related education, global education, social problems, values clarification, moral/citizenship education, and community participation programs. This trend represents a series of imaginative efforts by educators to specify more clearly parts of the citizen's role and to create instructional materials to enhance students' abilities in regard to that part of the citizen's role. Although they are not mutually exclusive or widely adopted by schools across the country, each of these approaches represents a somewhat different point of view.[6]

Third, citizenship education is a society-wide process.[7] Unlike many other areas of the school curriculum, citizenship is taught and learned not only in school but also in the community. Business, labor, voluntary organizations, religious organizations and the family all contribute formally and informally to citizenship education. For example, many community organizations such as the American Legion and the 4-H support or conduct their own citizenship education programs. At present, however, little is known about the relationship between citizenship education in school and nonschool settings and the extent to which efforts in different sectors reinforce or contradict each other.

As a result of these conditions, there is a need for analytical "tools" or guidelines to help educators in school and nonschool settings identify basics, clarify goals, assess needs, and develop action plans related to citizenship education. This handbook is a problem-solving tool, not a new curriculum outline. Our goal is not to prescribe one course of study or instructional approach to citizenship education. Instead, it is to use existing knowledge to help bring clarity to a complex educational domain often characterized by frustrating ambiguity.

2. Basic Citizenship Competencies: A Summary

Citizenship concerns the rights, responsibilities, and tasks associated with governing the various groups to which a person belongs. What competencies do individuals need in order to discharge their responsibilities and protect their interests as citizens? In response to this question we have examined research, theory and practice related to political behavior and training. Our goal was to identify the types of citizenship competencies which were basic and useful to a wide variety of individuals interested in citizenship education. By useful we mean a typology of competencies that could be used by educators to identify what is fundamental in citizenship education, to make comparisons between different approaches to citizenship education and to identify instructional practices and materials likely to promote citizen competence.

What do we mean by *basic* citizenship competencies? Considerable public attention has been given to the need for a return to "basics" in education. Educators have responded in a variety of ways. Today, there is disagreement and even confusion about the meaning of "basic" in education. By *basic* we mean a set of citizenship competencies that have these characteristics:

—They are limited in number.

—They are close to being universally relevant in that they are linked to citizenship tasks all individuals—regardless of sex, race, ethnicity, social class, or other differences—face in some form in the course of daily living.

—They are generic in that they apply to all of the various domains (family, school, city, state, nation, etc.) in which an individual may exercise citizenship.

—They should be taught continually in all grade levels at increasing levels of sophistication and variety.

—They are of the greatest value to individuals as they strive to discharge their responsibilities, to preserve their rights and to protect and pursue their interests as citizens.

—They are of value to the society as it seeks to maintain and improve itself.

We have identified seven citizenship competencies which meet these criteria. In a democratic society the exercise of these competencies should be constrained and tempered by a commitment to human rights and to democratic participation in the shaping and sharing of values. The competencies are:

1. *Acquiring and Using Information:*
Competence in acquiring and processing information about political situations.

2. *Assessing Involvement:*
Competence in assessing one's involvement and stake in political situations, issues, decisions and policies.

3

3. *Making Decisions:*
Competence in making thoughtful decisions regarding group governance and problems of citizenship.

4. *Making Judgments:*
Competence in developing and using standards such as justice, ethics, morality and practicality to make judgments about people, institutions, policies, and decisions.

5. *Communicating:*
Competence in communicating ideas to other citizens, decision makers, leaders and officials.

6. *Cooperating:*
Competence in cooperating and working with others in groups and organizations to achieve mutual goals.

7. *Promoting Interests:*
Competence in working with bureaucratically organized institutions in order to promote and protect one's interests and values.

These seven competencies should be looked upon as a set of flexible tools or guidelines for identifying what constitutes basic preparation for citizenship today. They are not intended to be a curriculum outline in and of themselves. In addition to these competencies, many other goals in citizenship/social studies/social science education can and should be pursued.

The competencies meet our criteria for *basic* in these ways: First, they are limited in number. Second, they are universally relevant in the sense that all individuals—white or black, rich or poor, young or old—require some level of proficiency with such competencies if they are to be responsible and effective citizens in the various groups to which they belong. Of course, such factors as great wealth can make it easier and/or less necessary for a person to exercise these competencies. By the same token, racial prejudice or sexism can make it more difficult for some to develop and exercise such competencies. Nevertheless, these competencies are relevant to most individuals under most circumstances.

Third, the competencies are generic. They cut across and apply to all of the various domains in which citizenship is exercised. People face the task, for instance, of making decisions about governance not only as citizens of the United States but also as members of their state, community, school or family. Similarly, effective participation in the life of a family, labor union or city may require the citizen to cooperate with others or make judgments about the decisions of others.

Fourth, the competencies can and should be developed continuously from the earliest stages of learning throughout life. These competencies are relevant to elementary-school-age children in settings encompassed largely by their interpersonal relations with parents, teachers, principals, peers, older children and various adults. As children mature, they develop both emotionally and cognitively, and the relationship of the individual to the social environment changes. Hence, as they grow older, students will exercise these competencies in an increasingly wider variety of political settings. These settings will eventually directly involve governmental institutions and citizenship as it relates to community and nation.

Fifth, these competencies embody the types of behaviors that are necessary, if not always sufficient conditions, for preserving one's rights and protecting one's interests as a citizen. For example, while competence in communicating effectively with bureaucrats does not guarantee that one can obtain certain benefits, it is hard to imagine being able to obtain anything without some such competence.

Sixth, the distribution of these types of competencies across the population is likely to be of value to the society as a whole. Societies without significant numbers of citizens who can, for example, acquire information, make independent judgments and communicate their opinions to public officials are less likely to be able to maintain democratic traditions and forms of governance than societies with such individuals.

Finally, it should be noted that the seven competencies are interdependent. This means that to some extent proficiency with any one competence is related to proficiency with one or more of the others. Making decisions, for example, involves collecting information. Competence in protecting one's interests when dealing with a bureaucracy will be enhanced by competence in communicating effectively with officials and leaders.

★ ★ ★

Up to this point we have briefly described seven citizenship competencies. These competencies, along with the concept of citizenship, will all be discussed in more detail in the remainder of the handbook. The accompanying chart summarizes the competencies and the discussion to follow. The chart lists the seven competencies and the capacities which contribute to them in addition to providing examples of knowledge, skills and attitudes related to each capacity. These examples are intended only to illustrate the various traits associated with each competency; they do not define the knowledge, skills, and attitudes that make up each competency and the capacities associated with it.

Summary Chart of Citizenship Competencies*

COMPETENCE in . . .	Involves and is demonstrated by the capacity to . . .	which implies such knowledge, skills and attitudes as . . .
1. Acquiring and using information	1.1 use newspapers and magazines to obtain current information and opinions about issues and problems . . .	a. reading at an appropriate level; b. distinguishing the various parts of a newspaper or magazine (editorials, opinion columns, news stories); c. understanding possible sources of bias in news gathering and reporting; d. distinguishing statements of fact and value.
	1.2 use books, maps, charts, graphs and other sources . . .	a. reading at an appropriate level; b. identifying the most appropriate source(s) of information for a problem at hand; c. applying basic information processing skills (e.g., reading for the main idea; use of index headings and summaries) to the material.
	1.3 recognize the unique advantages and disadvantages of radio and television as sources of	a. understanding the role and nature of the media in the American economic system; b. distinguishing between

---

* The numbering system for the capacities does not imply a hierarchy among capacities. Thus, for example, capacity 1.6 should not be taken as more important than 1.3 or 1.5 nor do the numbers imply that 1.1 to 1.5 logically or developmentally precede 1.6.

information about issues and problems . . .

pseudo-events and real events.

1.4 identify and acquire information from public and private sources such as government agencies and community groups . . .

a. identifying the most appropriate source(s) of information from the problem at hand;
b. using appropriate channels and procedures to obtain needed information.

1.5 obtain information from fellow citizens by asking appropriate questions . . .

a. developing productive and relevant questions;
b. identifying the best person(s) to answer a given question;
c. selecting effective methods of communicating a question such as a letter, telephone interview or survey.

1.6 evaluate the validity and quality of information . . .

a. distinguishing normative and empirical statements;
b. understanding the nature of sampling;
c. understanding the nature and logic of evidence.

1.7 organize and use information collected . . .

a. making longitudinal and cross-sectional comparisons;
b. clarifying information according to consistent sets of criteria;
c. conceptualizing information by analyzing it, breaking larger concepts into subconcepts;
d. conceptualizing information by synthesis,

combining objects or
ideas into more inclu-
sive concepts;

e. making inferences
from available infor-
mation;

f. developing hypotheses
that assert a relation-
ship between two or
more variables;

g. imagining alternative
possibilities for exist-
ing realities;

h. evaluating the reli-
ability and validity of
information.

COMPETENCE in . . .	Involves and is demonstrated by the capacity to . . .	which implies such knowledge, skills and attitudes as . . .
2. Assessing involvement	2.1 identify a wide range of implications for an event or condition . . .	a. identifying several groups affected by an event or condition; b. seeing that an event or condition can have: multiple consequences, different consequences for different groups, different consequences for different values such as wealth, health, safety, etc.
	2.2 identify ways individual actions and beliefs can produce consequences . . .	a. empathizing with others and recognizing their needs, feelings and interests; b. holding others' interests as legitimate and valuable as one's own.

| | 2.3 identify your rights and obligations in a given situation . . . | a. taking a sociocentric rather than egocentric perspective;
b. identifying relationships among trends, changes, problems in a group;
c. seeing how individual acts can accumulate to produce consequences that are difficult to predict. |

COMPETENCE in . . .	Involves and is demonstrated by the capacity to . . .	which implies such knowledge, skills and attitudes as . . .
3. Making decisions	3.1 develop realistic alternatives . . .	a. collecting information relevant to the decision problem; b. imagining alternative possibilities for existing realities.
	3.2 identify the consequences of alternatives for self and others . . .	a. empathizing with others, and recognizing their needs and interests; b. taking other's interests as legitimate as one's own interests; c. looking ahead and recognizing that actions have consequences which can ramify and accumulate.
	3.3 determine goals or values involved in the decision . . .	a. identifying the values which are involved in a decision problem; b. clarifying which values are of greatest importance.

	3.4 assess the consequences of alternatives based on stated values or goals . . .	a. identifying the extent to which a consequence violates or reinforces a value.

COMPETENCE in . . .	Involves and is demonstrated by the capacity to . . .	which implies such knowledge, skills and attitudes as . . .
4. Making judgments	4.1 identify and, if necessary, develop appropriate criteria for making a judgment . . .	a. clarifying the purpose for which a judgment is being made; b. identifying one's beliefs and values relevant to the judgment problem; c. identifying and assessing the utility of "traditional wisdom" as a source of criteria.
	4.2 apply the criteria to known facts . . .	a. preparing a mental or written checklist of criteria; b. comparing the problem in terms of the items in the checklist.
	4.3 periodically reassess criteria . . .	a. using a variety of sources to collect information on the continuing relevance of criteria; b. judging whether criteria are workable in light of changing purposes and conditions.
	4.4 recognize that others may apply different criteria to a problem . . .	a. recognizing that people culturally different from oneself may have different standards; b. according legitimacy to standards different than one's own.

COMPETENCE in . . .	Involves and is demonstrated by the capacity to . . .	which implies such knowledge, skills and attitudes as . . .
5. Communicating	5.1 develop reasons supporting your point of view . . .	a. collecting information relevant to the problem at hand; b. logically organizing information to support one's position.
	5.2 present these viewpoints to friends, neighbors, and acquaintances . . .	a. speaking clearly and writing clearly; b. understanding the concerns and values of others.
	5.3 present these viewpoints in writing to public officials, political leaders and to newspapers and magazines . . .	a. identifying the appropriate audiences for one's message; b. identifying the most appropriate form and procedures for submitting messages to target audience; c. writing clearly.
	5.4 present these viewpoints at public meetings such as committees, school board meetings, city government sessions, etc.	a. identifying the procedures involved in submitting such a message to a particular group; b. speaking clearly.

COMPETENCE in . . .	Involves and is demonstrated by the capacity to . . .	which implies such knowledge, skills and attitudes as . . .
6. Cooperating with others	6.1 clearly present ideas about group tasks and problems . . .	a. organizing one's ideas and thoughts; b. presenting ideas in a logical and orderly fashion.
	6.2 take various roles in a group . . .	a. organizing and leading a discussion; b. listening carefully to the views of others.
	6.3 tolerate ambiguity . . .	a. seeing ambiguity and uncertainty as natural and inevitable; b. accepting the best solution or answer currently available while continuing to work on a problem.
	6.4 manage or cope with disagreement within a group . . .	a. seeing conflict as a natural and inevitable part of the human condition; b. identifying alternative ways to manage a conflict including withdrawal and compromise; c. seeing the moral complexities involved in a conflict in the sense that two conflicting parties may both have a legitimate basis for their position.
	6.5 interact with others using democratic principles . . .	a. seeing and treating others in nonegocentric ways;

		b. seeing and treating others in a nonethnocentric way; c. empathizing with others.
	6.6 work with others of different race, sex, culture, ethnicity, age and ideology.	a. avoiding stereotypic perceptions of others; b. seeing racial, cultural, sexual, ethnic and age-related diversity as natural and inevitable.

COMPETENCE in . . .	Involves and is demonstrated by the capacity to . . .	which implies such knowledge, skills and attitudes as . . .
7. Promoting interests	7.1 recognize personal interests and goals in a given situation . . .	a. asking "What do I want? What are my goals in this situation?"; b. distinguishing between long-term and short-term interests; c. recognizing what may be realistically achieved in any given situation.
	7.2 identify an appropriate strategy for a given situation . . .	a. recognizing there may be alternative ways to exert influence; b. calculating the costs and benefits of one strategy over another in terms of one's purposes.
	7.3 work through organized groups to support personal interests . . .	a. finding groups most relevant to the problem, situation or issue with which one is concerned;

b. arranging one's time
and responsibility to
allow for participation
in such groups.

7.4 use legal remedies
to protect personal
rights and
interests . . .

a. recognizing how and
when one's legal rights
are affected by a prob-
lem or issue;
b. identifying basic types
of legal procedures
which may be related
to the problem one is
dealing with, including
lawsuits, criminal pro-
cedures, and injunc-
tions;
c. identifying the principal legal institutions
and actors available to
an individual, includ-
ing lawyers, legal
clinics, and small
claims courts.

7.5 identify and use
the established
grievance proce-
dures within a
bureaucracy or
organization . . .

a. recognizing the nature
of bureaucracy;
b. locating sources of information on grievance
procedures.

3. The Components of Basic Citizenship Competencies

We have briefly summarized the most important characteristics of the seven competencies. And we have said that citizen competence is a primary goal of citizenship education. In this section we define citizenship competence and describe in detail each competency and specific capacities related to it.

The Meaning of Citizenship Competence

Competence is a familiar idea. In daily life we often make judgments about people's competence. We may say "he is a competent cook" or "she is a competent lawyer." But just what is competence?

Competence implies a capacity or ability equal to some requirement. It means an ability to do something well.[8] To say a person is competent means that he or she is qualified or able to perform in a way that meets a standard or requirement in a given situation. A competent trial lawyer, for example, is able to make cogent arguments and purposefully cross-examine witnesses in a courtroom situation. A competent cook can consistently produce nutritious and appetizing results in the kitchen. Of course, we are all familiar with the idea that the same person may be highly competent in one role and less competent in another. The competent lawyer may be a mediocre cook, and vice versa.

In the same sense that individuals can be more or less competent in executing tasks associated with a particular occupational role such as that of lawyer, cook, plumber, secretary or bricklayer, individuals can be more or less competent in coping with tasks of citizenship. Citizenship competence refers to the quality of a person's participation individually or with others in processes related to group governance such as making decisions, protecting one's interests, or communicating effectively with group leaders. This includes the capacity to act individually in one's own behalf and the capacity to act in concert with others. Thus, *by citizenship competencies we mean the particular capacities an individual requires if they are to behave in such a way, or use their efforts in such a manner, as to produce consequences they intend in their role as citizens.* In a democratic society, competence implies citizens will produce consequences which do not violate human rights and which are congruent with principles of liberty and justice.

Citizenship competence has both an individual and societal dimension. The individual dimension refers to the skills, abilities, motivations and knowledge developed by the individual as he or she matures. Thus competent citizens have the capacity to exercise leadership or communicate effectively when a given situation requires them to do so. Experience indicates some people are more competent as citizens than others.

The societal context of citizen competence refers to the extent to which institutional arrangements in a group permit or facilitate the exercise of individual capacities. An individual's competence in any given situation can be frustrated by social forces or conditions beyond their immediate control. Citizens, for example, have little opportunity to exercise their abilities as information processors in situations where institutions withhold information on public issues or provide only misleading information. Experience shows that some forms of governance and social conditions provide greater opportunity for the exercise of individual competencies than others.

Self-esteem. Self-esteem has an important relationship to citizenship competence.[9] Self-esteem involves a continuing series of self/other comparisons. For example, "I am smarter than John but not as smart as Mary." Self-esteem is one of the primary ways we locate ourselves in relation to others. One source of heightened self-esteem is the perception that one is good at doing something. Thus, increased self-esteem may result as a person develops citizenship competencies. Being good at the task of citizenship may lead to an increasingly positive self-evalution.

At the same time, a high level of self-esteem can increase the likelihood an individual will develop greater proficiency with citizenship competencies. Research, for instance, clearly indicates that persons with high self-esteem are more likely to participate in social events than persons with low self-esteem.[10] High levels of self-esteem then appear to facilitate the person's ability to both take part in and learn from their social environment. One implication for citizenship education is that learning experiences in any content area which promote the individual's self-esteem may indirectly contribute to the person's development of citizenship competencies.

Civic literacy. What some have termed *civic* or *political literacy* also has an important relationship to the development of citizenship competence. Civic literacy entails an understanding of the basic values of democratic society, knowledge of the operation of informal political processes and formal political institutions, and a continuing awareness of contemporary social issues, problems and conditions.

Civic literacy has both an independent and dependent relationship to the basic competencies we have described. That is, at any age level competence in the citizen's role implies an individual will have sufficient knowledge and understanding of the political environment to act effectively. At the same time, competent participation in civic and public life can enhance factual knowledge directly, deepen understanding and motivate the individual to acquire yet additional knowledge.

Seven Basic Citizenship Competencies and Sample Learning Experiences

We will now take a close look at the components of each of the seven competencies identified earlier. For each competency we will identify several *capacities*. These capacities help us operationalize the competency. The capacities describe behaviors associated with each competency. Specifying capacities provides a way to think about two questions regarding each competency. These are:

1. What experiences will give individuals the chance to acquire and to practice the competency?
2. What behavior will demonstrate the attainment of some level of proficiency with each competency?

The capacities we identify are not intended to be totally exhaustive. Under certain circumstances, with particular individuals, capacities other than those listed here may be involved in the exercise of a competency. In addition, the proficiency an individual may attain with any given competency and its related capacities will be constrained by the level of the individual's cognitive, emotional and perceptual development as well as by external factors in their social environment. The capacities we describe in turn involve complex mixes of knowledge, skills and attitudes. Such knowledge, skills and attitudes are generally identifiable but are likely to be uniquely configured in each individual.

For each competency we also identify illustrative learning experiences at each of several age/grade levels.* By learning experiences we mean planned exercises and activities wherein pupils interact with an instructional environment which may include a teacher and/or other adults, printed materials, and/or simulated or actual events. The sample learning experiences show that it is possible to provide competency-related instruction in school for individuals from the elementary grades through early adulthood. The examples increase in sophistication and complexity to mirror the expanding cognitive, emotional, social and physical maturation of learners.[11]

The sample learning experiences have not been field tested and are neither definitive nor the only instructional strategies for promoting each competency. Rather, they illustrate the kinds of learning experiences that could allow students to acquire and practice each competency. The learning experiences incorporate a wide variety of instructional techniques—such as case studies, role playing and group discussion—found in currently available social studies/citizenship materials.[12]

---

*The sample learning experiences for the primary grades were prepared by Dr. Barbara Winston, Northeastern Illinois University. The sample experiences for the intermediate grades were prepared by Dr. Charlotte Anderson, assistant director, Law and Humanities Project, American Bar Association. The middle and high school experiences were prepared by Dr. John J. Patrick, Indiana University.

Acquiring and Using Information

Competence in acquiring and processing information about political situations. This involves the capacity to:

Acquiring and Using Information

—Use newspapers and magazines to obtain current information and opinions about issues and problems.
—Use books, maps, charts, graphs and other sources.
—Recognize the unique advantages and disadvantages of radio and television as sources of information about issues and problems.
—Identify and acquire information from public and private sources such as government agencies and community groups.
—Obtain information from fellow citizens by asking appropriate questions.
—Evaluate the validity and quality of information.
—Organize and use information collected.

How can I learn what benefits I am entitled under the Medicare system? Is a permit needed to remodel a front porch? Is it really the case that violence in our school is on the rise? What are the legal rights and responsibilities of a poll watcher?

From an early age on all citizens need to acquire and use information about their political environment. Children, for example, require such competence as they strive to understand why there are often fights on the playground or whether the sixth-grade bullies will be hanging around Elm Street on the way to school. Adolescents may need such competence as they look for groups which may share their interests in ecology or as they seek to apply for a work permit. Adults need such competencies when they vote in a referendum on whether to lower property taxes.

Acquiring information means extracting information and data from the environment. Processing information means critically evaluating, organizing and sensibly using information. We may, of course, acquire information simply for the joy of the process or because some topic or problem interests us. In our citizen role, however, the mere collection of information is often not an especially useful end in itself. Rather, competent citizenship often requires that "information acquired should be used in some purposive manner leading to greater understanding of a situation, an entity, a problem or ideas about productive solutions."[13]

Processing information has become increasingly important. We live in an information-rich culture characterized by public issues that are highly complex and technological in nature. We are often submerged by a torrent of information: economic information on the latest move of the consumer price index or the unemployment rate; sociological information on crime, the divorce rate or smoking habits; opinion polls on politicians or race relations; census information about population shifts or trends in education.

Yet any advantage citizens today might have from this flow of information is frequently offset by the complexity of contemporary issues. For the combination of big institutions and sophisticated technology confront us with an array of technological questions undreamed of two decades, let alone two centuries, ago. Should, for example, the United States proceed with the development of nuclear power plants or divert resources to solar energy production? How will deregulation of natural gas affect the prices we pay for heating our homes? Thus in today's information-rich culture often the task facing the citizen is not to acquire additional information but rather to make sense out of and use the Niagara of data already pouring forth on complex topics and problems.

Competence in acquiring and processing information involves the capacity to use printed sources such as newspapers, magazines and books to obtain factual information and opinions about issues and problems. Such competence also involves the capacity to recognize the advantages and disadvantages of radio and television as sources of information, and the capacity to acquire information from sources such as government agencies and community groups. Finally, it involves the capacity to ask appropriate questions.

Competence in acquiring and processing information also requires the capacity to critically evaluate the validity and quality of information acquired. Frequently this information takes the form of assertions about the nature of reality or fact. Upon inquiring, for example, we are told that increasing taxes will help curb inflation, or that the United States is dangerously behind the Soviet Union in military strength. What are the facts?

The citizen's task in assessing the quality of informa-

Acquiring and Using Information

*Acquiring
and
Using
Information*

tion is often confounded by at least two factors. First, biased, inaccurate or misleading information may be intentionally or unintentionally presented to support a particular factual claim. Proponents, for example, of one or another public policy may present "objective" information which supports only the policy, regulation or legislative action that benefits them. Further, the same information can be and often is introduced to support very different or even contradictory policies.

Second, the technological nature of many issues today means that pertinent information may be highly technical and difficult for a layperson to interpret and evaluate. Confounding this fact is the problem that experts often disagree among themselves about the significance and quality of such technical information.

The capacity to evaluate information in turn involves specific abilities and understandings of the type associated with the process of social scientific inquiry. These include the ability to distinguish normative and empirical statements, some understanding of the logic of sampling, the ability to detect bias in data, some understanding of the nature of evidence and the like.

Finally, competence in acquiring and processing information requires the capacity to organize, store and use information in relation to given problems. This, in turn, involves specific abilities associated with critical thinking. These include: comparing, classifying, conceptualizing, inferring, hypothesizing, and imagining. To a considerable extent such thinking processes are interdependent; they cannot be separated. For example, when individuals classify complex data, they may make inferences and draw comparisons in order to categorize the information. Thus, in using any of the processes, individuals may summon one or all other intellectual operations.

Competence in acquiring and using information is related to all six other competencies. In particular, this competency will be enhanced by the capacities associated with competence in assessing one's involvement and stake in political situations (number 2) and by the capacities related to making judgments (number 4). At the same time, competence in information acquisition and processing is especially important to proficiency in making decisions (number 3), communicating effectively with others (number 5) and working effectively with bureaucratic institutions (number 6).[14]

The following learning experiences illustrate ways individuals can be helped to develop competence in acquiring and processing information about political situations
in their environment.

Primary Level (Grades K-3)

Students could interpret a teacher-drawn map that
shows how a family uses space in their home. Using the
map key, students identify spaces that adults use, spaces
that children use, and spaces that the whole family shares.
Then children sketch maps to show how space is divided
and shared in their own homes. Children's maps and the
teacher-drawn map can be compared to find similarities
and differences in ways families divide and share space.

*Acquiring
and
Using
Information*

★ ★ ★

Students could identify the best person to ask when
given a list of situations or questions and possible people
to go to, e.g.:

You Want to Know	The Best Person to Ask Is
1. When will the school gym be open?	Your mother The crossing guard The school nurse The school principal
2. What are the rules in the cafeteria?	A police officer The school nurse Your teacher
3. Where can I find out about the first school in our community?	The school librarian A police officer A baseball player
4. How do I report a fire or other emergency when I am home alone?	A little boy or girl Your parents

Intermediate Level (Grades 4-6)

Students could interview members of the city council

to find out what decisions they have made in the last year that directly affect the children in the community. For each "case," locate and review newspaper accounts and relevant council minutes to identify facts and issues. Answer such questions as: How does the council make decisions? Do the newspaper accounts adequately and accurately reflect the council deliberations as recorded in the minutes? What were the differing opinions expressed? What were the concerns of each interested party? Evaluate the council's decisions on the basis of criteria the students identify.

Acquiring and Using Information

* * *

Students could keep a record of the contents of the classroom wastebasket over several days. Record the information on a chart according to established categories; e.g., notebook paper, ditto sheets, candy/gum wrappers, pencils/crayons. At the end of the period, identify and compare the quantity discarded in each category. Discuss possible waste and ways of curbing the waste. Put this plan into action. Continue to record the discarded items for another period of time equal to the first. At the end of this time, compare findings with the first period. What changes are there? Are fewer items being discarded?

Junior High School Level (Grades 7-9)

Students can become more-competent finders of information by practice in using the index section of books. For example, learners might use the indexes in three U.S. history textbooks to locate all the references to Thomas Jefferson. Learners can practice the skill of information processing by organizing the findings about Jefferson into three lists: (1) contributions to achievement of American independence, (2) achievements as a public official, and (3) achievements as a scholar and writer.

Grade 10-Adult

Focus the attention of learners on a current public issue that has divided the community. For example, banning or restricting the use of throw-away bottles has been an important issue in many communities. Ask learners to construct a set of questions to uncover public opinions

about the issues. Then have learners administer the
questionnaire to a representative sample of respondents.
After gathering these public opinion data, learners can
organize, interpret and report their findings.

*Acquiring
and
Using
Information*

Assessing Involvement

Competence in assessing one's involvement and stake in political situations, issues, decisions and policies. This involves the capacity to:

Assessing Involvement

—Identify a wide range of implications for an event or condition.

—Identify ways in which individual actions and beliefs can produce consequences.

—Identify one's rights and obligations in a given situation.

Will defeat of the school bond issue affect property values in my neighborhood? Does it matter that my fellow team members want to elect the captains next year rather than let the coach choose them? How might a change of government in the Middle East affect the family plan to drive to the West Coast next summer? Does it matter whether I report the crime just witnessed? Do I have an obligation to attend the next committee meeting? City officials want to prohibit smoking in public places; what are my rights?

Competence in assessing one's involvement in political situations is important in itself. Some people, while walking through a forest, see nothing. Others perceive the variety of plants, detect growth and decay, observe signs of birds, mammals, insects, and evolutionary history in the rocks around them. Citizens who can perceive the richness of the political forest around them are more able to protect and promote their interests than citizens who cannot. Such competence, for example, can help an individual make choices about when in cost/benefit terms participation is worth the effort. In addition, this competence is often a necessary condition for proficiency with other competencies such as making judgments, acquiring information, and making decisions.

Assessing one's involvement and stake in political situations means identifying the consequences for self and others that may stem from political events and conditions and identifying the implications for others of one's own actions, values, beliefs and feelings.

Events or conditions have an impact on individuals when they have an effect on one's personal circumstances or physical well-being in such terms as wealth, health, safety and the like. Decisions, for example, regarding food and drug laws may affect one's health. Policies regarding taxation may affect one's wealth. The creation of a civilian review board for a police force may affect one's safety, rights and liberties.

Events or conditions also have an impact on individuals when they affect the person's sense of humanity in terms of their sense of moral integrity, ethical commitment, spiritual commonality with fellow humans, pride, or patriotism. Discrimination against Jews in Russia is an event likely to be perceived in such ways. Such events may have no immediate or direct impact on one's own physical well-being, but their indirect effect on us may be very real nevertheless.

Assessing Involvement

Competently assessing one's involvement or stake in group life requires a capacity to identify the implications of an event or policy. Does, for example, the decision to build a superhighway through town affect only those whose homes will be lost, or does it also have an impact on merchants, trucking companies, paving contractors and engineers, among others? The more groups an individual perceives to be affected by an event or condition, the greater the chance that person will be a member of such a group, and hence discover how such events or conditions can have a personal effect.

Competence in assessing one's stake in political situations also involves a capacity to identify ways in which individual actions and beliefs produce consequences in small and large group settings. The competent citizen can see the relationship between his or her actions in a small group and group welfare. For example, the competent union member sees the potential relationship between economic welfare, declining union memberships, and a steward's request for help with a recruitment drive next Saturday night. Competence involves the capacity to see how individual behavior has consequences for large groups by aggregating or accumulating to produce often unintended consequences for oneself and others. The competent citizen can see, for example, how failure to report a crime is not an isolated act but rather a behavior which, if repeated by many citizens in a community, can lead to a decrease in safety for all.

Finally, competence in assessing one's involvement in group life involves the capacity to identify one's rights and obligations in a given political situation. Rights are

Assessing Involvement

prerogatives and protections to which a person is entitled by virtue of human nature and membership in a group. Obligations are duties or responsibilities which flow from membership in a group. Obligations may be legally or socially imposed. Citizenship in a group implies a reciprocal relationship between rights and obligations. As one political scientist explains, "Citizenship thus is conceived as a condition of reciprocity . . . in which one both enjoys rights and performs duties, in which liberties are mutually balanced by obligations."[15]

Competence in assessing one's involvement and stake in political situations is enhanced by competence in acquiring information and making judgments. At the same time, competence in assessing involvement contributes to all the other basic competencies, particularly competence in making decisions (number 3), working with others (number 6) and promoting one's interests (number 7).

The following learning experiences illustrate ways in which individuals can be helped to develop competence in assessing their involvement and stake in political situations, issues, decisions and policies.

Primary Level (Grades K-3)

Students could imagine what school would be like if there were no rules (about running, raising one's hand, taking responsibility for one's supplies, etc.). Children draw pictures or write stories to show how they and other children and adults in the school would be affected by the imaginary situation. Pictures or stories can be discussed to identify the people affected and ways in which they were affected by the imagined condition. Children can then discuss the value of given rules.

* * *

The students could listen to or read short stories which present dilemmas such as the following: "The teacher has just told the children that $2.00 is missing from the Red Cross collection. Jane saw two children playing with the money while the teacher was out of the room. What should Jane do?" After reading each dilemma story, the children should be directed to identify alternatives open to the person, note the possible consequences of following each suggested course, and determine the best action considering the interests of both the group and the individuals involved.

Intermediate Level (Grades 4-6)

Students could develop a plan for each classroom to assume responsibility to clean up the school playground, cafeteria, gymnasium, halls or classrooms. The plan could also involve monitoring safety, decorating an area, improving order, etc. The students should then prepare a poster with the names of people assigned to each job so that obligations are recognized. The governing council presents awards at the end of the year to good citizens who fulfilled their obligations. They should also evaluate overall consequences of the plan, identify its weaknesses and strengths, and make recommendations for the following year.

Assessing Involvement

★ ★ ★

Students could use graphs that show available quantities of a given resource (fuel, metals, forested land, etc.) and graphs that show use of that resource by people in the U.S. in 1930 and 1970. Students project quantities for the graphs during the year 2000. Discuss implications with students if the present trends continue. Have them suggest reasons why they might wish to change the trends and make specific recommendations on how their own behaviors and the behaviors of others might help to accomplish this.

Junior High School Level (Grades 7-9)

Present brief examples of decisions by policymakers in local and national governments in this country and in other countries. For example, one might describe a decision by a local government to ban smoking in public places. Or a decision by a Middle Eastern government to cut oil production and raise prices might be described. Divide learners into small groups of four or five. Then engage them in a brainstorming discussion in which they offer speculative responses to two questions: (1) How might the decision affect me? (2) How might it affect various others? Challenge each small group to generate as many valid responses as possible within a specified period of time. Then have the groups report their responses to others in the class and defend them.

Grade 10-Adult

Assessing Involvement

Assign the task of keeping a journal, for one week, to describe political decisions reported in local news media. In addition, ask learners to note in their journals any policy decisions they have experienced directly during the week. Tell learners to assess their stakes in each decision by noting how the decisions might affect them and various others.

Making Decisions

Competence in making thoughtful decisions regarding group governance and problems of citizenship. This involves the capacity to:

—Develop realistic alternatives.
—Identify the consequences of alternatives for self and others.
—Determine goals or values involved in a decision.
—Assess the consequences of alternatives based on stated values or goals.

Making Decisions

Should I vote for candidate X or candidate Y in the next election? Should I join with my fellow students in protesting the high school's new parking regulations? Should we support the principal's new staff development program? Should I attend the public hearing on rezoning the land next to the new school?

Decision making is an inescapable part of citizenship for young and old alike.[16] Children require decision-making competence when they must choose a leader for a playground game or decide whether or not to break a school rule. Adolescents need decision-making competence when a problem requires them to choose between loyalty to their peers and loyalty to their family. Adults need such competence when they choose local, state and national political leaders.

A decision is a choice from among two or more alternatives. As individual citizens, we constantly face the task of making choices from among many possible alternative courses of action. In addition, we often cooperate or take part with others in group decision-making activities. For example, when we serve on a committee or vote in an election we are taking part in a group decision-making process.

Over a lifetime citizens face an incredible variety of decisions regarding phenomena, problems and processes of group governance. These include selecting leaders; deciding how to manage or resolve conflicts or disagreements; choosing ways to handle the effects of interdependence, such as a gasoline shortage; determining what rules to make, how to allocate benefits, what goals to set.

Three enduring decision problems faced by young and old alike have to do with loyalty, compliance or support,

*Making
Decisions*

and participation in group life. These enduring dilemmas of citizenship are: (1) Under what conditions should I (as citizen of a family, a city, a nation, or the global community) be loyal to or proud of my group, and when should I be critical? (2) Under what conditions should I (as citizen of a given group) actively participate in the political life of the group and, if necessary, sacrifice for the common good, and when should I defend or assert my private interests or withdraw to nurture my private life? (3) Under what conditions should I (as a citizen of a given group) comply with the laws, rules or norms of that group and support its political authorities, and when should I defy rules and authority?

Thoughtful decision making involves a conscious search for alternatives and assessment of the consequences of alternatives in light of the decision maker's values or preferred goals. Thoughtful decision makers take account of the impact of their choices on both self and the group. Consideration of both facts and values is involved in thoughtful decision making.

Facts are involved in the identification and consideration of alternatives and their consequences. Should, for example, the principal make rules that restrict individual rights but promote orderly behavior? In part, the decision involves gathering and evaluating information about facts. How unruly are students? What evidence is there that proposed remedies will have any effect? Are there legal implications in limiting students' speech?

Values and value judgments are also a critical part of thoughtful citizenship decision making.[17] The thoughtful decision maker makes value judgments when labeling consequences as negative or positive. While establishing goals, the thoughtful decision maker engages in clarification of values and ethical reasoning. Such clarification involves asking, "What is important, what do I want, and what is right or wrong in this situation?" Citizen decision makers who lack the capacity to clarify and analyze their values may establish goals or choose alternatives that contradict their own or democratic values.

Thoughtful decision making related to group governance involves several capacities: to identify alternative courses of action, to determine important values or goals affecting the decision and to consider the positive and negative consequences of alternatives in terms of stated goals or values.

Competence in making decisions clearly involves several other competencies. In particular, decision-making competence will be enhanced by competence in acquiring and using information (number 1), in assessing one's involvement in political situations (number 2) and in using appropriate standards to make judgments (number 4).

The following learning experiences illustrate ways in which individuals can be helped to develop competence in making thoughtful decisions regarding group governance and enduring dilemmas of citizenship.

Making Decisions

Primary Level (K-3)

Students could look at pictures showing two or more children faced with a problem situation (a child chasing a ball into the street and a car approaching, a kite caught in a tree, an animal trapped in a burning house). Children identify the problem, generate alternative solutions to the problem, evaluate consequences of each alternative in terms of their own welfare and the welfare of others, and decide on a course of action with a rationale.

★ ★ ★

The students could look at pictures of children responding in different ways to the same choice situation. Describe the situation and the way each is responding. Tell what seems to be important to each child as suggested by their behavior. Evaluate the responses on the basis of criteria established and suggest other possible responses. Consider own responses in similar situation. Such a sequence of pictures might show: (1) a small child who has fallen off a tricycle and is sitting next to the fallen bike, crying; (2) another child running past the fallen child to flag down an ice cream truck; (3) still another running by to join a ball game, and (4) a third child stopping to comfort and help the crying child.

Intermediate Level (Grades 4-6)

Students could evaluate a state highway department's proposal that a new highway should be built through a large park. The department's arguments say that the proposal would be the cheapest possible plan, since the route is the shortest between two cities and the park land is government-owned. Students identify groups that might be affected by the decision (taxpayers, families with homes around the park, wildlife groups, people who use the park for recreation or study, etc.), and role play how each group might feel about the proposal. Students decide if the highway department's proposal should be supported or whether alternative proposal(s) would be preferable, and present reasons for their decisions.

★ ★ ★

Making Decisions

Students could establish criteria needed to make a decision about a class party, a field trip, or a speaker. Groups of children discuss alternative ways to carry out the activity and present suggestions to the class. The whole group votes on a plan based on one or more proposals consistent with established criteria.

Junior High School Level (Grades 7-9)

Students can sharpen decision-making skills by keeping a log of important decisions made during one week. They can be required to chart these decisions by identifying alternatives, likely consequences of each alternative, and their goals in each occasion for decision. Finally, students can reveal their choices in each instance, why they made the choice, and whether or not they are satisfied with the outcome.

Grade 10-Adult

Decision-making skills can be practiced through analyses of realistic cases of group governance. For example, learners can read a case study about public officials who are trying to decide whether to ban swimming in a large lake. The city health officer has presented evidence of pollution in the lake that might be dangerous to the health of swimmers. However, the city's businesses, which depend on tourist trade, could be severely damaged if the council decides to ban swimming. Furthermore, the pollution levels are not so high that the danger to the swimmers is certain. In this case, the city council faces a decision in which basic environmental and public health values are in conflict with basic economic values. Learners can be asked to analyze this case, make a justifiable decision and then defend it in discussion with other learners.

Making Judgments

Competence in developing and using such standards as justice, ethics, morality and practicality to make judgments about people, institutions, policies, and decisions. This involves the capacity to:

—Identify and, if necessary, develop appropriate criteria for making a judgment.
—Apply the criteria to known facts.
—Periodically reassess criteria.
—Recognize that others may apply different criteria to a problem.

Making Judgments

Is it fair for the teacher to cancel recess because several kids were talking during the spelling lesson? Was the mayor's decision to buy new snowplows a wise use of tax money? What criteria should we use to judge whether the proposal to locate a nuclear power plant in our county is good or bad? How should we evaluate the performance of our club's officers last year?

Making judgments is one of the most pervasive tasks of citizenship. Competence in making judgments is required when citizens evaluate whether it was a mistake for the president to veto a new law or students determine whether it is unfair that the city prohibits bike riding on city sidewalks. Such competence is also required when citizens must determine what judgment criteria or standards to use in a situation. Does, for example, one evaluate a court's decision to permit a neo-Nazi march in terms of individual liberties, public safety or yet other criteria?

Judgments involve evaluative activity. Judgments are claims about the goodness or badness, the desirability or undesirability, the appropriateness or inappropriateness of given phenomena. To judge a person, institution, policy or decision is to weigh its worth in terms of some set of criteria. Judgments may be rigorous, take a long time, involve an elaborate set of criteria, be based on limited data or intuition, and be made quickly.

Criteria are standards or rules for making judgments; they are assertions about the qualities, characteristics or properties in terms of which a phenomenon will be judged. Criteria help individuals evaluate and determine the worth of something. For example, the use of majority

Making Judgments

rule is one criterion for judging whether a group makes decisions democratically. As individuals develop into adult citizens they learn criteria to make many different judgments associated with the citizen role. These are, in effect, "ready-made" criteria, and they make it easy for people to make judgments quickly. For example, individuals learn that honesty is a standard for judging the worth of a political candidate. Some people are more aware or conscious than others that they are using criteria when they make judgments as citizens. Conscious use of criteria can result in more effective citizen judgment making.

Competent citizens will use criteria which are consistent with their purposes and values. Thus, competence in making judgments involves the capacity to consciously identify (and develop, if necessary) criteria for making judgments that reflect one's needs and values. For example, competent citizens who value the arts and culture will not judge a candidate's qualifications for public office solely in terms of the candidate's physical appearance. Rather, they will use criteria related to the candidate's past record in support of the arts as at least one important criterion for judgment. Establishing criteria is the value phase of making judgments; this process reflects the individual's claim about the values in terms of which a phenomenon should be judged.

Competence in making judgments involves the capacity to apply criteria systematically to a given issue or problem. When applying criteria the individual assesses the extent to which the phenomenon being judged does or does not possess or measure up to the desired qualities, characteristics or properties reflected in one's criteria. Applying criteria is the performance phase of making judgments, in that we appraise the "performance" of a policy in terms of individual criteria.

Primary Level (Grades K-3)

Students could generate a list of criteria for judging the arrangement of their own classroom and explain why each is important. This list may include such criteria as: is safe, looks nice, has places for people to do different things. Place students in small groups to build models of the room based on established criteria. Present, compare, and evaluate individual models. Arrange the classroom according to one of the most highly rated models. After a period of time, reevaluate this arrangement; make appropriate adjustments. Do the criteria still stand? Are others needed?

★ ★ ★

Students could generate a list of several things they like to do (a range of activities such as running, resting, climbing, digging, reading, eating, etc.). They observe various rooms in the school to see which of their favorite activities would be appropriate for the spaces available. As they observe each room and make suggestions for possible activities, children provide reasons why an observed space might be more appropriate for one activity than another (e.g., the gym is better than the classroom for running because there is more space, there are fewer obstacles, running is allowed, etc.).

Making Judgments

Intermediate Level (Grades 4-6)

Students could use a graph that shows amounts of money spent in one year by the U.S. government on health, education, military expenses, and aid to foreign countries. Discuss the information on the graph and designate groups of students to assume the following roles and write letters to the government: a school principal, a doctor, a person from a country where people do not have enough to eat, a military leader. Have students read their completed letters aloud and discuss reasons for similarities and differences in their opinions.

★ ★ ★

Students could imagine that they are sign painters for a multinational corporation with factories in Nairobi, Paris, Madrid, Tokyo, and Brazil. Their task is to prepare signs for use in *every* factory to communicate such messages as "No Parking," "Visitors Welcome," "No Smoking," "Turn Out the Lights," etc. Assign two groups of students to work on one message, two more groups on another message, and so on. Each group should design the most effective way to carry out the task. Students show completed signs while others guess the messages. Through discussion, students see the relevant criteria for judging the sign (whether it communicates the message and can be used in all locations) and see that there may be more than one "right" way to communicate the same message.

Junior High School Level (Grades 7-9)

Making Judgments

Students could be asked to formulate in writing one standard, or criterion, for justifying each one of several choices encountered in daily living, such as buying a pair of shoes, selecting players in a pick-up basketball game, or casting a vote in a public election. Then learners can be paired and asked to report and justify their criteria to their partners.

Grade 10-Adult

Learners could complete a written exercise in which they formulate, justify, and apply a set of criteria for judging the performance of personalities and/or institutions. For example, they might be asked to use criteria to judge the role behavior of a public official, a candidate for public office, or a salesperson advertising a product. Begin the lesson by having each learner select an object for appraisal. Then require the learner to formulate and justify at least three criteria by which to judge the object. Finally, have the learner rate the object in terms of the criteria and justify the rating in an oral report.

Communicating

Competence in communicating ideas to other citizens, deci-
sion makers, leaders and officials. This involves the capacity
to:

—Develop reasons supporting one's point of view.
—Present these viewpoints to friends, neighbors, and
acquaintances.
—Present these viewpoints in writing to public officials, political leaders and to newspapers and
magazines.
—Present these viewpoints at public meetings, such as
committees, school board meetings, and city government
sessions.

Maria wants her 4-H club to enter a project in the
county fair; she stands up in a club meeting to argue for
her position. A group of high school students encounter
the assistant principal in the hall and discuss ideas for an
after-school gym program; the assistant principal asks
them to "put their ideas in writing." Tom is asked by his
neighborhood association to testify at the next city council meeting.

Competence in communicating one's ideas to others is
an essential part of citizenship in a democracy. Children
and adolescents require such competence when they seek
to influence the decisions of their peers or when they
participate in school or club activities. Adults may need
such competence when they try to influence the decision
of a public official or when they need to provide information in order to obtain benefits from or deal with a
bureaucracy.

The term *communicating* is used here in the narrow
sense of passing along or transmitting ideas and information to others in either written or oral form. Communicating as described here may or may not involve two-way
interaction between the communicator and the intended
recipient of information. In one sense, formulating an
argument and presenting it effectively has always been a
task of citizenship. In another sense, communicating information and ideas to officials and political leaders has
become increasingly challenging as the scale of society
and the complexity of issues have increased. Today one
may need or wish to communicate with officials in a be-

wildering array of agencies far removed from one's immediate community. Often, communicating with such officials involves coping with esoteric jargon and a cobweb of regulations and procedures.

Competence in communicating with others involves the capacity to construct an argument representing one's point of view. It further involves the capacity to present information and/or one's argument to others in writing or orally. And it involves the capacity to accomplish personal presentations in either informal settings with neighbors and acquaintances or in such public arenas as school board and city council meetings.

Communicating

Proficiency with this competence will be greatly facilitated by competence in acquiring and processing information (number 1) as well as by competence in making judgments (number 4). At the same time, facility in communicating information to others can enhance one's competence in cooperating and working with others (number 6), and one's competence in working effectively with bureaucratically organized institutions (number 7).

The following learning experiences indicate ways in which individuals could be helped to develop competence in communicating their ideas to fellow citizens and decision makers, leaders and officials.

Primary Level (Grades K-3)

The students could discuss possible ways of resolving some problem in the classroom. For example, if people are not hanging up their coats and putting their boots away properly when they come in in the morning and after recess, what should be done about it? After allowing time for students to think about responses, have everyone sit in a circle and listen to each person present his or her position in turn. After everyone has had an opportunity to speak, identify each of the reasons why each proposed solution is good and not so good. On the basis of these reasons, decide what the class should do and why. Agree to follow the decision of the group.

★ ★ ★

Students could identify an issue in the school (gum on desks, a clean-up problem, or another relatively simple issue). They should seek information about the problem with special attention to who is affected and who will be affected by its resolution. Students should then solicit opinions about resolving the issue from a reasonable sample of concerned individuals or groups. Based on information from interviews, students construct and present arguments to the student governing body.

Intermediate Level (Grades 4-6)

Students could study a relevant problem in the community. After study, students decide on their positions relative to the problem and prepare supportive arguments to defend their viewpoints. Identify the appropriate means for presenting arguments (letters, orally, etc.), and decide to whom the arguments should be presented. Follow through by making oral and/or written presentations to designated audiences.

Communicating

Junior High School Level (Grades 7-9)

Assign students to look at the letters-to-the-editor section of a local newspaper for a one-or two-week period. Tell each student to select one letter which takes a stand about a current issue and try to criticize the letter writer's position. Have the learner write a letter to the editor to rebut the letter he or she has challenged in class.

Grade 10-Adult

Require learners to use newspapers, TV newscasts, and radio news programs as sources of information about a current issue before their state legislature or city council. Have them chart the decision-making situation and arrive at a defensible choice. Then have each person draft a letter to communicate his or her opinion on the issue to a representative in the state legislature or city council. Ask the students to exchange drafts with partners, and let one person in every pair critique the partner's letter in terms of previously taught criteria for writing letters to public officials. Conclude the lesson by having learners write final drafts of their letters, taking into account the partner's criticisms, and sending the letters to their representatives in the state legislature or city council.

Cooperating

Competence in cooperating and working with others in groups and organizations to achieve mutual goals. This involves the capacity to:

Cooperating

—Clearly present ideas about group tasks and problems.
—Take various roles in a group.
—Tolerate ambiguity.
—Manage or cope with disagreement within the group.
—Interact with others using democratic principles.
—Work with others of different race, sex, culture, ethnicity, age and ideology.

Steve has been selected as the fifth-grade safety patrol captain and now must work with other patrol members to devise next week's schedule. Carlos wants to continue working as a volunteer with the local court-watching project but he disagrees with many of the project director's ideas. Sheila has gotten most of her fellow tenants to go along with the idea of a rent strike—now they look to her for continued leadership.

Much of the citizenship and politics of daily life occurs in relation to the governance of such groups as the family, school, the work place, and voluntary organizations. In addition, participation in the governance of larger groups often occurs through the medium of such small groups as councils, task forces, committees and the like. Competence in cooperating and working with others is required when a student is appointed to a group planning the class picnic. It is also exercised when high school students organize a demonstration in support of a popular teacher who was dismissed. Similarly, such competence is displayed when a group of adults form a committee to distribute petitions required to get a candidate's name on a ballot in a local election.

This competence involves a range of human relations and self-management capacities requisite to relating effectively to others. These capacities have a distinctly affective dimension. They entail attitudes and emotional orientations associated with ways people interact with each other. These capacities are the capacity to clearly present one's ideas in written or oral form, to take

various roles in a group, to tolerate ambiguity, to manage
conflict, and to guide one's interaction with others by
democratic principles.

This last capacity—to apply democratic principles—
deserves special attention. Democratic citizenship means
a commitment to the dignity of all individuals and the
preservation of the values of life, liberty and property. In
a democracy these rights are seen as inalienable; that is,
they were not given to individuals by governments, and
no government may legitimately take them away. Democratic citizenship also means commitment to equal opportunity for all people to develop their individual
capacities.

Cooperating

Competence in this regard, however, does not mean
abstract commitment to these ideals but the *application*
of these ideals in dealing with others in daily life. For
adults this means relating to and making decisions about
others in group settings in nonegocentric, nonethnocen-
tric and nonstereotypic ways. Neither a teacher nor a
parent should be very satisfied with students who can
recite the Golden Rule and the Bill of Rights accurately
but who consistently infringe on the rights of those
around them.

The National Council for the Social Studies' revised
curriculum guidelines emphasize this point:

> This century has witnessed countless blatant violations
> of human dignity in the presence of supposedly well-
> educated populaces. It has been frequently asserted that
> knowledge is power; however, there is little evidence to
> assert that people who know what is true will do what is
> considered right. Commitment to human dignity must
> put the power of knowledge to use in the service of
> humanity.[18]

Finally, it should be noted that while self-esteem is
related to all the basic citizenship competencies, it probably bears a special relationship to this competency.
Research consistently affirms that self-esteem is fundamental to active citizenship in small group settings:
"if an individual feels worthless and ineffective, he or
she will perceive that there is nothing to be gained by
becoming involved."[19]

Competence in working with others will be enhanced
by proficiency with making decisions (number 3) and in
making judgments (number 4). At the same time, this

competence can enhance one's competence in protecting one's interests (number 7). Often the most effective way to promote and protect one's interests is to join forces with others with similar interests.

The following are illustrations of learning experiences which can help individuals develop competence in cooperating and working with others in group and organizational settings in order to achieve goals.

Cooperating

Primary Level (Grades K-3)

Students could role play a problem situation involving a child and adult. The problem should incorporate both (1) a responsibility for the child (doing the dishes, cleaning up the art table, erasing the board, etc.) and (2) the child's desire to do something "legitimate" other than his or her responsibility (play baseball with the team, do a homework assignment, help a friend fix a wagon, etc.). After children understand the problem, have them role play alternative solutions including the following examples: (1) compromise, (2) the adult "giving up," (3) the child "giving up." Discuss the consequences of each solution.

* * *

Students could look at pictures that show ways in which family members depend on one another. Pictures should show children depending on adults (for protection, to learn, etc.), and adults depending on children (for love and affection, to learn, to do chores, etc.). Then each child draws one picture showing how adults in families depend on children and another picture showing how children depend on adults.

Intermediate Level (Grades 4-6)

Students could observe the teacher leading a demonstration discussion. After discussing the roles of the leader and the participants, the students form small groups with student discussion leaders. An observer assigned to each group reports at the close of the discussion on what the group did. After considering what might be done differently, new leaders are identified and the process is repeated, focusing on a new topic.

* * *

Let students use case studies to practice identifying and evaluating alternative means of managing conflict that grows out of group membership. The following is a useful case: "A group of girls built a clubhouse in Erica's backyard. Ann and Pam brought all the lumber, and everyone worked to make the clubhouse. After the clubhouse was finished, Erica took a new way home from school. When she passed the lumberyard, she heard two people talking about the lumber that was missing—$100 worth, from the pile out in front! Erica's heart jumped into her throat. Where did Ann and Pam get all that beautiful new lumber? What should she do now?"

Cooperating

Junior High School Level (Grades 7-9)

Organize students into small groups of four or five members. Give each group the task of planning and carrying out a certain classroom assignment, such as creating a bulletin-board display; organizing and conducting a classroom discussion on a current topic of interest to the group; choosing, inviting, and hosting a guest speaker on a current topic; or organizing and conducting a classroom social event. One inviolate requirement of each small-group activity is that every group member must make a tangible and significant contribution to achieving the group's goals. Conclude the lesson by conducting a debriefing discussion focused on problems and successes in cooperating to achieve a group goal.

Grade 10-Adult

Require small groups of learners, four or five members to a group, to identify, plan, and carry out a community service project, such as an antilitter campaign in the school or community, a fund-raising project to provide money for a local charity, or a get-out-the-vote drive in a neighborhood during an election campaign. Have participants keep a log of their experiences. Finally, have them report and debrief their experiences in a discussion with other learners.

Promoting Interests

Competence in working with bureaucratically organized institutions in order to promote and protect one's interests and values. This involves the capacity to:

—Recognize one's interests and goals in a given situation.

—Identify an appropriate strategy for a given situation.

—Work through organized groups to support one's interests.

—Identify and use established grievance procedures within a bureaucracy or organization.

A fourth-grader talks with friends about how to get into the "neatest" activities at summer camp. A teenager registers with the Bureau of Motor Vehicles in order to obtain a driver's license and in the same week visits his father's union office to learn how to qualify for college scholarship benefits available from the union. A group of irate homeowners files a complaint with the state insurance commission against a disreputable property insurance company.

Contemporary society is marked by the growth of large institutions that have an increasing influence on our daily lives.[20] Along with the growth of big government and big business in modern life has come an increase in professionalism, technocratic decision making and bureaucracy in the political and economic sectors of society. When organizations reach a certain size, whether they are schools, summer camps, corporations, universities, labor unions or government, they take on universal bureaucratic characteristics. These characteristics include specialization or division of labor; hierarchy, or fixed lines of command; and job security incentives to attract workers and build their loyalty. In turn, such characteristics are usually understood to lead to impersonality, devotion to rules at the cost of individual values, rigidity, too much paper work and red tape.

Competence in dealing effectively with bureaucratically organized institutions is increasingly a part of citizenship. Citizens acting individually and with others interact with these large, bureaucratically organized institutions in two ways. First, we are consumers or recipients of public services and products of such organiza-

tions—particularly of government institutions. There
has been a tremendous growth of the role of government
in providing goods and services since the end of World
War II. Today, local, state and national government provides electricity through government-owned utilities,
inspects the food we eat and the medicines we use, provides weather forecasts via satellites, finances low-
interest mortgages, operates school buses, provides
welfare payments and food stamps, trains the handi-
capped, runs hospitals, sets health and safety regulations, regulates the stock market and so on.

*Promoting
Interests*

Government provision of services is part of a societal
movement toward a "service/consumer society" in
which society-related work and the consumption of service are replacing manufacturing as primary factors.
Social scientists explain that the basic framework of the
emerging service society is a political economy
characterized by a tremendous expansion occurring in
health, education and welfare services and in government employment.[21]

Second, citizens increasingly look to various government agencies to promote their interests, values and
causes. Thus, for example, blacks, Mexican Americans
and American Indians may look to the Department of
Justice to promote their civil rights. Citizens concerned
with the quality of the environment attempt to promote
their interests through federal, state and local environmental agencies.

Competence in working with bureaucratically organized
institutions involves a range of capacities: to identify
one's interests and goals in a given situation, to identify
an appropriate influence strategy or tactic in a given
situation, to use organized groups to support one's rights
and interests.

Thus, a competent citizen could determine whether it
would be more appropriate to work with a lawyer or a
doctor to obtain Medicare benefits which were unfairly
denied. A competent citizen would recognize the value
of finding an interest group such as a local consumer
organization which supported his or her values in a given
conflict. Competent citizens would know how to enlist
legal assistance (e.g., small-claims court, a legal clinic)
when necessary to protect their rights.

Competence in dealing with bureaucratic organizations is enhanced by several other competencies,

especially competence in assessing involvement (number 2), making decisions and judgments (numbers 3 and 4) and communicating with others (number 5).

The following learning experiences illustrate how individuals can be helped to develop competence in working effectively with bureaucratically organized institutions in order to promote and protect their interests and values.

Promoting Interests

Primary Level (Grades K-3)

The students could identify problems in the school which directly affect them. Find out if there are any rules which should be preventing the problem. If so, devise strategies to have the rules more effectively enforced. If not, devise strategies to establish rules to correct the situation. For example, some third-graders are unhappy because the older students are always using the monkey bars at recess, with the result that they never get a chance to play on the monkey bars.

* * *

The students could identify, role play and evaluate alternative ways to exert influence when assuming the role of the central character in such cases as the following: (1) Mary Jane's family is trying to decide whether to go to the zoo or a ball game this weekend—Mary Jane wants to go to a ball game; (2) Dick's teacher has told the class they can decide whether to have math first in the morning or after recess—Dick wants math first; (3) Barbara's club is trying to decide how to spend the money they have earned mowing yards—Barbara thinks half the money should go to charity.

Intermediate Level (Grades 4-6)

The students could organize a club. Working together as a group, they could decide what will be the purpose of the club, identify other potential members and have a membership drive. During the first club meetings they could determine what activities the club members will participate in and what the dues will be and elect officers.

* * *

Students could investigate a problem in the community. After doing research on the problem, they can determine the position the group will take, identify other community groups which are likely to support that position, and invite these groups to join in a cooperative effort to influence other citizens and community officials. They could then evaluate such alternative strategies as making posters, writing letters, holding public informational meetings or demonstrations, and conducting a telephone campaign. A possible problem might be children crossing unsafe streets on the way to school, limited and inaccessible recreational facilities, abandoned and unsafe buildings in which children are playing, or too many dogs running loose and scaring children.

*Promoting
Interests*

Junior High School Level (Grades 7-9)

Present tips for effective citizen action in influencing public officials. For example, indicate how to use the law to influence bureaucrats or how to use ombudsmen of the type provided by certain metropolitan newspapers or television stations. Then have students apply tips for influencing public officials to the analysis of case studies of citizens faced with problems of dealing with recalcitrant or incompetent bureaucrats. Ask students to devise strategies for solving the citizen's problem in each case.

Grade 10-Adult

Have learners "map" a local bureaucratic agency to find out who does what, how the agency works, whom to see to obtain different services, who has certain kinds of decision-making authority, etc. Some of this information can be obtained from an organizational chart of the agency. Other information might be obtained through interviews of personnel within the agency. Finally, information may be obtained through interviews of some of the agency's clients and from recent newspaper stories about the agency. Conclude the lesson by having learners report on how the agency functions and how to obtain various services.

Testing for Citizenship Competencies

The citizenship competencies described here represent guidelines for establishing desired goals or outcomes in citizenship education. This typology of competencies can help educators clarify their goals in the area and assess the degree to which their current programming teaches basic skills that individuals need as children and as adults.

Can these competencies be reliably and validly measured through minimum-competency-testing programs or state and national assessments? The question is important because there is a growing concern for minimum competency testing. So far, 36 states have set up testing programs to measure student skills in such areas as reading, writing and mathematics. Nine of these states have included citizenship as one of the areas in which competency should be demonstrated.*

Research and experience indicate that it may be very difficult to meaningfully test large numbers of students for important citizenship competencies and to interpret test results, once obtained. There are special considerations involved in measuring citizenship competencies which do not apply equally to such areas as science, mathematics, reading and writing.

Difficulty in mass-scale testing of citizenship competencies arises from the fact that—unlike the sciences, reading and writing—some of the most important citizenship competencies involve human relations and social skills which are difficult to measure using paper-and-pencil tests. Yet, at present, practical considerations all but require the use of paper-and-pencil tests in minimum-competency-testing programs. As a result, some of the most important citizenship competencies—making decisions, making judgments, working with others—are difficult to reliably and validly measure.

When such testing is attempted, important competencies or objectives are often reduced to trivial aspects of the citizen role. The result is that schools, teachers and programs are assessed in terms of those aspects of citizenship competence which can easily be measured, even though the importance of what is being measured is inversely related to its measurability.

Difficulties in interpreting citizenship test scores stem from the nature of the political learning process through which citizenship competencies are developed. Research indicates that political learning is a society-wide process affected by many "agents" or societal forces in addition to the schools. Individuals can and do acquire citizenship-related knowledge, skills, attitudes and values on the street, in the home, from television, and from peers as well as from teachers and classes in school.

In contrast, while nonschool forces can affect a student's ability to learn other subjects, we do not expect the mass media or peer groups to teach students physics, chemistry, writing or mathematics. In today's society these educational tasks have become largely delegated to the school.

The implication of the society-wide nature of citizenship education is that

---

*These are California, Georgia, Missouri, North Carolina, Oregon, Utah, Vermont, Virginia and Wyoming.[22]

when students are given citizenship competency tests it may be difficult to attribute variance in test scores to school and nonschool factors. In other words, it is difficult to determine the contribution to students' scores of the school as opposed to the home, peers, television, and the like. The National Assessment of Educational Progress recently faced this problem. Results from a recent citizenship/social studies assessment of junior and senior high students showed that students' knowledge of basic legal rights had increased since the last assessment. However, it was very difficult to ascertain to what extent this outcome was attributable to increased exposure to police-oriented television shows or to increased efforts at legal education in the schools.

Competency testing is often advocated as a means of forcing greater accountability upon the schools. However, given prevailing competency-testing and assessment techniques, there is presently little reason to believe that such testing can help educators, policymakers or parents make more-informed judgments about the contribution of the schools to teaching basic citizenship competencies.

However, difficulties of the type just described do not mean that teachers and curriculum supervisors working closely with students in classroom settings cannot evaluate student progress in developing basic citizenship competencies; quite the contrary. Good teaching must include procedures for determining whether instruction has been successful in helping students achieve desired changes in competence. These procedures should be an integral, continuing part of the instructional process. Such instructional theorists as Davies, Popham and Baker, and Patrick consider in detail the theory and practice associated with assessing instruction and learning.[23]

A variety of appraisal strategies is likely to be necessary to assess student achievement of knowledge, skills and attitudes pertinent to basic citizenship competencies. These strategies would certainly include paper-and-pencil tests. In addition, however, appraisal would likely require somewhat less-familiar techniques, among them teacher observation of student performance in real and/or simulated settings and student self-reports and diaries. The ultimate goal of all such appraisal of student learning should be to help teachers and curriculum developers improve their instructional techniques and materials.

4. Criteria for Learning Experiences That Promote Citizenship Competencies

I hear and I forget. I see and I remember. I do and I understand—Old Chinese proverb

The basic citizenship competencies described in this handbook must be developed by actual practice and active learning. As with any set of skills, the more opportunities individuals have to practice, reflect on and demonstrate their citizenship competencies, the more likely it is that they will develop proficiency in them. Carl Rogers put it clearly: "Significant learning is acquired through doing."[24]

The case of learning to ride a bicycle is instructive. To develop such competence, a person must have the experience of actually riding a bicycle under a variety of conditions. One may prepare for the experience and contribute to one's proficiency by studying the physics involved in bicycle riding, by learning safety rules or by studying the design of bicycles. Parents can structure the learning experience to increase the probability of success by providing advance instructions, training wheels, the proper size and type of bicycle, a safe area to ride, feedback on progress and remedial instruction. But without continued practice, there is little likelihood that one will ever become a competent bicycle rider.

Similarly, to develop competence in citizenship decision making a person must have the experience of actually making thoughtful decisions under a variety of conditions. The learner may prepare for the experience and contribute to proficiency by learning the rules of formal decision theory or by studying the lives of great decision makers. Educators and parents can facilitate learning by providing appropriate decision problems, opportunities to practice making decisions without unduly suffering their full repercussions, and appropriate feedback and instruction. But, as with bicycle riding, learners must have repeated experiences with actually making choices if they are to become competent decision makers.

Thus, both practice and actual experience play a key role in developing citizenship competencies. The question for educators, parents and community leaders is: What kind of learning experiences will give students the opportunity to exercise and practice citizenship competencies in order to improve their level of proficiency and demonstrate attainment of competence? Such experiences are not confined to formal schooling; in fact, the schools may not be the only nor the best institutions for providing some types of learning experiences.

In this section we consider four criteria for evaluating citizenship learning experiences. These criteria can serve as standards or tests for the design, implementation, and evaluation of citizenship learning experiences. They are drawn from theory and research on sound principles of instructional design. Learning experiences which meet or conform to these criteria will be more beneficial than learning experiences which do not. Learning experiences can be created and curricula can be compared in terms of these guidelines.

Citizenship learning experiences should incorporate reflection or debriefing by the learners. Debriefing or reflection by students on their experiences is critically important. Such reflection builds self-consciousness into the learning experience. It is the necessary bridge between the "raw" experience and the individual's capacity to learn from that experience. Debriefing may take many forms, including hypothesis testing, group discussion, and written or oral reports. The key component is self-analysis on the part of the learner.

Citizenship learning experiences should be related to the experiences of learners so that they perceive them as meaningful. Learning information and skills within a meaningful social context enhances both achievement and retention of learning.[25] Citizenship learning experiences should be made personally meaningful for students by being related to students' experiences with teachers, other school personnel, peers, older students and various adults in their community. Learning experiences can and should draw upon the political phenomena students encounter daily as citizens of the family, school and community.[26]

At the same time, citizenship learning experiences should extend students' horizons. Students who learn only in terms of immediate experiences are likely to be less capable than those with expanded horizons. Thus, learning experiences should also expose learners to new ideas and information and enable them to generalize from familiar and personally meaningful events to situations outside their immediate experience. Adequate citizenship learning experiences enable students to increasingly expand the range of political situations and events that may be perceived as meaningful to them.

Citizenship learning experiences should provide for cumulative reinforcement without boring repetition. Learning experiences should provide repeated opportunities for students to develop and practice basic competencies and associated abilities. Thus, learning experiences should allow for continuous practice, reflection and application in ways suitable to the cognitive, emotional and physical attributes of the learner at varying age/grade levels.

To the extent possible, learning experiences also should link capacities and abilities developed in one lesson or area of the curriculum to other lessons in different subject areas. The more connections that can be made between knowledge and skills developed in one learning experience and the competencies taught through other learning experiences, the more powerful the experience—the more one can do with the learning gained from it. Forging connections between learning experiences reinforces prior learning and also fosters new achievements.[27]

Citizenship learning experiences should encourage active competency learning. Learning experiences should be arranged so that students actively perform cognitive tasks directly related to the citizenship competencies they are learning about. For example, students should not only read about making decisions, they should practice actually making decisions. Active learning may be accomplished through real events, simulations, games or other instructional strategies. The key is student application of knowledge and skills to the completion of various tasks directly related to one or more basic citizenship competencies.

Such prominent learning theorists as Dewey, Bremer, and Rogers stress the importance of students' being involved as active learners. Dewey put it this way: "Only in education, never in the life of the farmer, physician, laboratory experimenter, does knowledge mean primarily a store of information aloof from doing." Piaget explained: "A truth is never truly assimulated except insofar as it has first been reconstituted or rediscovered by some activity." Such activity "may begin with physical motions" but comes to include "the most completely interiorized operations."[28]

5. Diagnosis and Prescription: A Checklist for Citizenship Competencies

The typology of citizenship competencies and criteria for learning experiences described in this handbook may be applied to specific curriculum problems and needs through the checklist described in this section. The checklist may be used by supervisiors, individual teachers or groups of teachers to:

—*make thoughtful comparisons* across many citizenship education/social studies materials;

—*assess existing goals, objectives and classroom instruction* in terms of basic citizenship competencies; and

—*set new goals* based upon inquiry and analysis.

A complete blank checklist is presented in the Appendix in the form of a blackline master.* The checklist may be reproduced in quantity and/or made into a set of transparencies for workshops and meetings.

The checklist is divided into five columns. The first column lists the citizenship competencies and related capacities described in this handbook.

The second column, titled "Materials," may be used to examine the extent to which instructional materials cover and promote competency-related capacities. If the textbook or set of materials includes opportunities for students to learn or practice a capacity, this should be indicated by placing an "X" in the "Yes" column; if not, the "X" should be placed in the "No" column. If the materials are found to provide capacity-building learning opportunities, those opportunities should then be evaluated in terms of the four criteria presented in the "Materials" column. The four criteria are drawn from the discussion of criteria for learning experiences in Chapter 4. In summary, they are:

—*Provision for reflection and debriefing:* Good instruction incorporates reflection and debriefing which involves the learner in considering in some manner the essential meaning of the learning experience.

—*Personal meaningfulness:* Good instruction connects to the experiences of learners so they perceive them as relevant.

—*Provision for reinforcement:* Good instruction provides for cumulative reinforcement without boring repetition.

—*Provision for application:* Good instruction encourages active learning wherein students apply what they have learned to new problems.

*The checklist described in this section was developed by the author and by Dr. Mary Jane Turner, codirector of the Basic Citizenship Competencies Project. Dr. Turner is a member of the Graduate Faculty of Education at the University of Colorado and a staff associate of the Social Science Education Consortium, Inc.

Citizenship Competencies Checklist

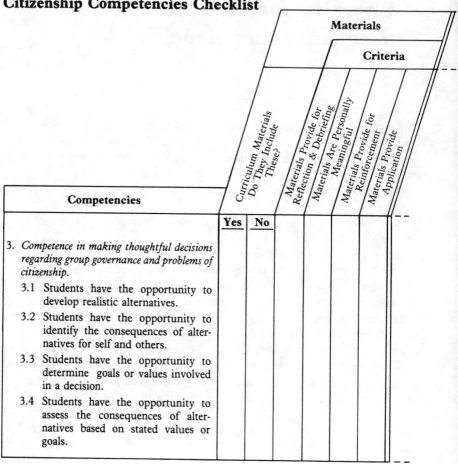

Competencies	Curriculum Materials Do They Include These?		Materials Provide for Reflection & Debriefing	Materials Are Personally Meaningful	Materials Provide for Reinforcement	Materials Provide Application
	Yes	No				
3. *Competence in making thoughtful decisions regarding group governance and problems of citizenship.*						
3.1 Students have the opportunity to develop realistic alternatives.						
3.2 Students have the opportunity to identify the consequences of alternatives for self and others.						
3.3 Students have the opportunity to determine goals or values involved in a decision.						
3.4 Students have the opportunity to assess the consequences of alternatives based on stated values or goals.						

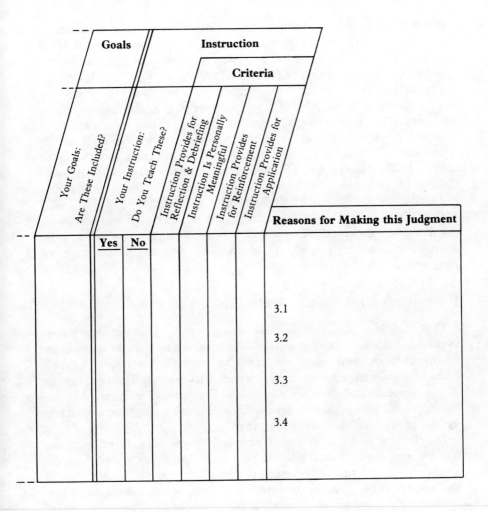

If it is believed that a capacity-building learning opportunity meets one or more of these criteria, an "X' should be place in the appropriate column. If the learning opportunity is present but does not meet a particular criterion, the column for that criterion should be left blank.

The third column, headed "Goals," refers to statements of objectives in instructional materials, the goals of a given teacher or group of teachers, grade-level goals, school district goals and the like. This column may be used by simply marking a "Yes" or "No" in the appropriate spaces in the column.

The fourth column, headed "Instruction," may be used in the same fashion as the "Materials" column. This column refers to classroom instruction—the combination of teacher-led and teacher-initiated activities, instructional materials and teacher response to those materials.

The fifth column, headed "Reasons...," provides an opportunity and incentive for users of the checklist to justify their ratings of materials, goals and/or instruction. This activity can often be as valuable as assigning ratings in a given category.

Examining Curriculum Materials

The "Materials" column of the checklist may be used by individuals or groups to examine a single textbook in order to determine how many of the competence-related capacities are included in the content. A book or other set of materials found weak with respect to particular competencies might still be a good choice if it is supplemented by other materials or instructional activities. In other words, one outcome of examining instructional materials with the checklist is to identify gaps which might need to be covered.

The checklist may also be used to compare the quality of several textbooks. The checklist can help users systematically determine not only which texts are weak or strong in a summative sense but also the areas in which their strengths and weaknesses lie. This may be particularly useful at textbook adoption time, when many sets of curriculum materials and textbooks are under consideration. Using a single analysis system such as the checklist means that many persons can be involved in the materials-selection task. Furthermore, if all materials regardless of content area are assessed in terms of the quality of the citizenship learning experiences they provide, it is more likely that such basic competencies will be consistently taught and reinforced at all grade levels.

Setting Goals

The "Goals" column of the checklist may be used to appraise the extent to which basic citizenship competencies are reflected in an individual teacher's, school's or school district's goals. Such an appraisal can be used as the basis for setting new goals to remedy deficiencies. Once an appraisal has been made, many different kinds of goals can be set.

One school might decide to emphasize citizenship education at four grade levels. A science department might choose to include or emphasize capacities related to competence in acquiring information, making judgments and communicating information. A school district might wish to provide inservice for all teachers focused on ways to structure learning experiences in which students actively practice citizenship capacities. Another district might involve elementary teachers in improving the quality of their citizenship instruction the first year, junior high school teachers the second year, and senior high school teachers the third year. A district might also decide to assess the quality of district goals and objectives and write new ones to include all of the basic citizenship competencies.

Assessing Classroom Instruction

The way in which content is taught can have a critical impact on students' citizenship competence. The column of the checklist titled "Instruction" can be a useful device for helping teachers diagnose strengths and weaknesses in their own teaching. Individual teachers can engage in self-assessments. At the same time, schools, grade levels and school districts can also engage in assessing classroom instruction. Identifying areas and degrees of strength and weakness is important in order to answer questions about differences in performance. For example, if all first-grade teachers are experiencing more success than second-grade teachers, the reason may be that the materials used in the second grade are not adequate. Or perhaps district goals and objectives do not emphasize citizenship capacities for the second grade. Careful diagnosis and comparison allow such decisions to be made deliberately and with full knowledge.

Using the checklist to assess classroom climate and instruction may be particularly helpful in evaluating cross-departmental instruction. Traditionally, citizenship has been a goal of all schooling, at all levels and in all departments. In practice, of course, education for citizenship has come to be largely concentrated in that portion of the curriculum assigned to social studies. This situation is appropriate with respect to content dealing with such topics as the structure of government and the history of the United States. On the other hand, all teachers, regardless of their subject-matter responsibilities, can affect their students' development of basic citizenship competencies by the way in which they carry out their teaching. In that sense, citizenship competencies and their related capacities transcend content areas.

Numerical Scoring of the Checklist (Optional)

It is possible to use a numerical scoring procedure with the checklist. This procedure may also be used to compare textbooks and curriculum materials, assess instructional programs, and set goals. Instructions for numerical scoring, along with scoring sheets, are presented in the Appendix.

Numerical scores are simply one way to help summarize judgments about the extent to which materials or instruction promote competencies. The scores are derived from subjective, professional judgments about quality. Individual judgments about the extent to which a particular capacity is developed by a text-book or classroom instruction will often vary. Thus, one should not be led into a false sense of security about the precision of such scores. For example, while there is clearly a significant difference between scores of .25 and .75, there is probably no significant difference between a score of .23 and one of .27.

Although using numerical scoring has limitations, doing so may serve several useful purposes. Scores can be used to (1) facilitate comparison, (2) give an indication of the relative strengths and weaknesses of materials or instructional programs, (3) provide a convenient summary of professional judgments, and (4) provide base-line information against which to assess progress and measure attainment of new goals.

6. A Working Definition of Citizenship for Educators

The basic competencies described in this handbook are anchored in and derived from a broad, rather than narrow, conception of citizenship. It is useful to make this distinction because as interest in citizenship education has grown, both educators and policymakers have found the concept of citizenship to be ambiguous. This ambiguity, in turn, has frequently led to difficulty in identifying the focus of citizenship education programs.

One alternative is to view citizenship narrowly in terms of the individual's relationships with formal institutions and processes of government at the local, state and national levels; individuals are assumed to be acting as citizens only when they are dealing with governments in some way or other. This definition has the advantages of precision and a kind of attractive simplicity. However, it also has disadvantages for educators concerned with preparing young people for competent membership in society, both as students and as adults.

Such a narrow conception of citizenship largely overlooks the political interactions which occur in daily life in such settings as homes, schools and clubs. As a result, citizenship is perceived as being largely divorced from the experiential world of all but the oldest students. Educational programs based on this narrow view of citizenship are not likely to be personally meaningful for students; they tend to treat students as passive learners who are not yet participants in governmental institutions. A narrowly legalistic definition of citizenship does not take into account the fact that, today, important values are often authoritatively determined by large nongovernmental organizations. Finally, the narrow definition is not congruent with the conceptions held by many teachers and parents who think of citizenship as being related somehow to student behavior in many different domains.

Another alternative has been to view citizenship as related to the totality of human sociability. In a word, the status of citizen is seen as a complex intertwining of the personal, social, anthropological and ecological dimensions of human identity. In the popular version of this view, the term *citizenship* is often used to refer to practically all prosocial behavior. One difficulty with such a broad view is that one quickly finds that the concept is of little use for developing instructional programs and making curriculum decisions. Citizenship viewed so broadly loses all empirical referent and comes to include everything and hence nothing.

The inherent ambiguity in the citizenship concept can be resolved to some extent by considering the following key characteristics of citizenship in today's society:[29]

—Citizenship is exercised in relation to governing or managing a group. Thus, while citizenship is an inherent part of human sociability, not all social behavior is citizenship behavior.

—Citizenship is exercised in relation to many types of groups, including but not limited to cities, states and nation.

—Citizenship is exercised by young and old alike and involves a wide range of decisions, judgments and actions which include more than such adult activities as voting, paying taxes and obeying laws.

—Citizenship involves participation in group life, but the relationship of participation to citizenship is complex. For example, there is not necessarily a direct relationship between "good citizenship" and political participation.

—Citizenship behavior in large groups, such as nations, is linked to issues of group governance through *aggregative processes.* For example, the supply of energy for a nation is not a direct result of decisions made by any one citizen. The availability and price of energy are, rather, cumulative consequences of aggregating the energy-related decisions and actions of millions of citizens.[30]

—Citizenship is increasingly exercised in an international or global context.

With these characteristics in mind, the following is a useful working definition of citizenship for educators: *Citizenship involves the rights, responsibilities and tasks associated with governing the various groups to which a person belongs.* These groups may include families, churches, labor unions, schools and private associations as well as cities, states, the nation and the global system. As members of these groups, young people as well as adults are involved—directly or indirectly, knowingly or unknowingly—in citizenship problems and tasks associated with participation in group life. As the basic citizenship competencies indicate, this conception of citizenship implies that the task of citizenship education is not simply one of preparing the young for a future adult role. Nor is it simply a task of teaching facts and loyalties relevant to governmental institutions.

Governance as a Central Feature of the Citizenship Role

The notion of *governance* is fundamental to concepts of both citizenship and political life. All groups must govern themselves in some fashion in order to survive. Schools must make rules for student and faculty behavior, city dwellers must decide whether to increase taxes or reduce services, and community club members must decide whether to raise dues. Citizenship behavior can be distinguished from other types of social behavior because it occurs in relation to such problems of governance.

Some groups, such as cities or nation-states, have over time evolved specialized political institutions which have responsibility for the governance of the group. In Western society these include city councils, parliaments, legislatures, dictatorships, courts, armed forces, regulatory agencies and bureaucracies. Of course, other social institutions—particularly economic institutions, such as large corporations—may make decisions and policies which affect the welfare of larger groups. Such policies may in turn create governance problems. Thus, a large corporation may close a factory in a town. The consequences of this action (unemployment, loss of tax revenue, etc.) may cause new governance problems for the city (how to combat unemployment, attract new industry, etc.).

Governance in other groups—for example, a family, labor union or a voluntary association—may occur in less-formalized ways. Some groups may not have evolved highly specialized routines and roles for handling such jobs as setting goals or making and enforcing rules for the group. Nevertheless, all groups face the fundamental political problem of governing themselves.

The way a group governs itself affects how such values as wealth, safety, and power are created and shared among members of a group. As one noted social scientist put it, politics determines "who gets what, when and how."[31] This is the case whether we are talking about the governance of the family, the school or the nation.

Choices are made concerning the governance of a classroom, for example, when an elementary teacher decides which students can operate the audiovisual equipment. Some students will have the pleasure of operating the equipment; others will not. A city council's decision to build a new library on the east side is also a governance choice. This means that people on the east side of town will have easier access to entertainment and enlightenment than people on the west side.

Group governance is accomplished through processes which are authoritative. Authoritative processes are collectively binding; that is, potentially enforceable for all members of the group. Thus we can say that *political situations within a group are those situations that involve phenomena, problems and processes associated with governance of the group.*

The basic *phenomena* associated with group governance are decision making, conflict, authority, change and interdependence. These phenomena are repeatedly experienced by young and old alike. They are present at all levels and domains of citizenship. Individuals confront these phenomena as they wrestle with problems of governance in their families, schools, labor unions, cities, states and nations. For example, individuals often face the task of making, judging or influencing decisions; they often have to manage conflicts; they must resolve who has authority; they must deal with the effects of change.

The basic *problems* associated with group governance include coping with disparities between political ideals and political realities, balancing political rights and responsibilities, and controlling the abuse of power. Some examples of related questions are: Why is political authority necessary? How do political decisions affect me and other people? How can I influence political decisions? What is a good or just political decision? What are my political rights? What are my political responsibilities and obligations?

The basic *processes* associated with political life and governance are making rules for the group, distributing resources within the group and setting group goals. Examples of rule making include allowing 18-year-olds to vote, prohibiting running in the school halls, and establishing a 55-mile-per-hour speed limit on highways. Examples of distributing resources within a group include establishing a social security system for citizens and giving some teachers more supplies than others. Examples of goal setting include deciding to lower the inflation rate or to establish minimum competency levels for graduation in a school district.

Citizenship in Various Kinds of Groups

Citizenship is not exercised only in relation to institutions of government. Rather, citizenship behavior occurs in relation to a school, a social club, or a labor union as well as in relation to a city or nation. Thus there are many domains or arenas for the exercise of citizenship. As one scholar put it, "There is no citizenship in general. It exists only in the particular domains of one's life."[32]

As a result, citizenship behavior is a very complex phenomenon. Social scientists have yet to clearly untangle the nature of the connections between citizenship behavior and practices in different domains or arenas. For example, it remains unclear to what extent active participation in governance problems in one domain (such as a school) prepares individuals for more-effective participation in another realm (such as a work place or nation). It is possible, however, to identify attributes and characteristics that are relevant to one domain of citizenship (such as knowledge of the by-laws of one's social club) and other attributes that are generic, which cut across the various domains in which we exercise citizenship (such as the ability to make thoughtful judgments). Our concern in this handbook is with such generic attributes of citizenship.

Citizenship for Youth and Adults

Citizenship is not something that only adults "do." The fact that citizenship involves governance issues in many groups means that citizenship education can and should do more than simply prepare the young for an adult role. It is possible to identify rights, responsibilities and tasks of citizenship which children and adolescents encounter in the course of their relations with parents, teachers, other school personnel, peers, and a wide variety of adults in neighborhood and community settings.

In their daily interactions with peers and adults, youngsters deal with the problems of political life. Rule making, for example, is found when a group of students create new rules for a social club or a class reaches an agreement about what behavior will and will not be permitted at its daily meeting. Conflict and its resolution, to take another example, is found in a fight between two children over the possession of a toy, in a playground argument about the rules of game, or in a dispute between a teacher and a student.

Unfortunately, this immediate dimension of citizenship has not been a chief concern of traditional civics programs. Citizenship and politics is treated as something that children can study from a distance and for which they can prepare, but in which they cannot participate until they reach the age of majority and become voters, taxpayers, campaign workers, public officials or candidates for electoral office. However, it should be clear from our discussion that citizenship learning experiences for students do not have to be confined to experiences associated with governmental institutions at the city, state and national level.

The Importance of Participation

The notion of citizenship clearly implies taking part in the political life of a group. However, the relationship between citizenship and participation is complex and goes beyond either simple exhortations that "all good citizens must participate actively" or that participation by large numbers of people is a clear sign of democracy at work. As to the latter point, we only need remind ourselves that massive citizen participation has been the hallmark of such societies as Nazi Germany and the People's Republic of China.

Useful or desirable citizen participation may encompass a wide range of behavior undertaken for an equally wide range of reasons. In any group, whether it be a city or social club, some members will want to participate by assuming very active roles in which they hold office, lead discussions, set agendas and the like. Such individuals often have a clear sense of responsibility along with a sense of purpose aimed at gaining certain benefits or protecting specific interests. Such participation may also suit their personality needs; it may be thought of as an enjoyable activity akin to sports, card playing and other forms of social diversion.

But most people participate less actively by simply supporting or complying through voting, obeying the law, paying dues or taxes and keeping themselves generally informed about current affairs within the group. Participation at such a level may be an indicator of apathy, alienation or deficient citizenship, but it may also simply reflect a realistic appraisal of one's power position in a group, a reasonable trust in the performance of existing leaders or a personality syndrome which is less extroverted than that displayed by more-active group members.

The point is that, under certain circumstances, good citizens can be informed followers as well as leaders or activists. As for group welfare, some political theorists and contemporary social scientists argue that massive participation can be a mixed blessing which can introduce instability and turmoil into group life. For example, there are circumstances when greater participation increases the intensity of social conflict. One political scientist asked: "Would a society in which every member was a vigorously outspoken activist be one in which enough agreement could ever be reached to accomplish anything?"[33] A classic dilemma in political theory revolves around the tradeoffs between efficiency in group decision making based on limited participation of citizens and the positive values obtained from wide-scale participation in such processes. Our purpose here is not to resolve such complex issues regarding citizen participation but simply to call attention to the fact that, while participation in political affairs is a key dimension of citizenship, there is not always a simple one-to-one relationship between active participation and either "good citizenship" or group welfare.

The Cumulative Effects of Individual Behavior

In large groups, such as a city or nation, people's behavior as citizens is linked to problems of governance and public affairs through aggregative processes. This means that individual actions, decisions and judgments have not only immediate, short-term, foreseeable consequences but also longer-term effects that often become apparent only when individual behavior is added together or aggregated with the behavior of thousands or millions of other citizens.

Political scientist Lee Anderson explains the aggregative process this way: Imagine an individual walking on a public street who observes a crime and does nothing either to aid the victim or to alert the police. The individual's inaction affects the distribution of an important value within his city; namely, security from violence. The direct and immediate consequence of inaction is readily apparent: the victim is left unaided. But there would also be systemic or aggregate consequences of such behavior if it were repeated by many other citizens. As indifference to crime increases, the frequency of crime is likely to rise and the level of security from crime enjoyed by all members of the community will tend to decrease. This, in turn, may pose new governance problems for the community involving curfews, the allocation of resources for additional police and the like.[34]

In short, the linkage between individual behavior and group governance may be direct and readily apparent in such small, face-to-face groups as families, clubs and classrooms. In large, impersonal groups, aggregative processes link the individual to the public affairs and governance of the group.

The Global Dimension of Citizenship

The competencies described in this handbook are exercised by citizens in an increasingly global environment. Although some might wish otherwise, the effects of global interdependence have become inescapable for all citizens. Global interdependence is a condition that must be dealt with, not merely a theory about other people's problems. International-relations scholar Chadwick Alger has pointed out that when we observe our own daily life we quickly become aware of how we are linked to a variety of international processes. In a single day the "typical" U.S. citizen, for instance, may be awakened by a Japanese clock radio, drink morning coffee from Brazil, drive to work in a Fiat on tires made of Malayan rubber, buy Saudi Arabian gas, and listen on a German-made radio to a news report about a visiting Bolivian trade delegation.[35]

Our contacts with the rest of the world are not limited to our lives as consumers. Money put into a savings account at a local bank is reinvested in an apartment complex in Chile. A donation in a church collection plate helps to build a hospital in Nigeria. Modern data-processing facilities permit scientists in Columbus, Ohio, Geneva, Switzerland, and several African cities to quickly exchange data on biological controls for insects harmful to people. A business investment in a local industry helps produce weapons that kill people in distant lands.

In short, global interrelationships that substantially affect the lives of all U.S. residents have gone far beyond traditional diplomatic negotiations and distant military confrontations. Our proliferating ties to nations, communities, peoples and events in other parts of the world affect the quality of our air and water; the price of sugar, coffee, and gasoline; the size of our armed forces; the amount of taxes we pay; the levels of employment and inflation. Similarly, how U.S. citizens behave affects the lives of others elsewhere. Our decisions and actions as citizens involve us in housing policy in Chile, health care in Nigeria, international scientific networks and death in far-off places. They link our lives to the lives of Japanese factory workers, laborers on Malayan rubber plantations and corporate executives in Germany and Italy.

Despite growing attention to global influences on the human condition, we are only beginning to appreciate the impact of this change on our lives as citizens and on the task of citizenship education. At minimum, people now confront the tasks and responsibilities of citizenship in a global or international context. Longshoremen, for example, decide whether or not to load U.S. grain on ships bound for Russia, or a group of business leaders seeks to influence a state legislature to provide financial inducements to foreign companies to locate in their state, or members of a university committee vote to restrict programs for foreign students, or local church members judge it unfair that church policy toward the world food problem is set by their national headquarters rather than being individually determined in each diocese. Thus, effectively exercising the seven competencies described in this handbook may increasingly require attention to citizenship responsibilities in the context of many territorial units in addition to the context of the nation. It may involve, for the first time in human history, not only an awareness of physically proximate neighbors but also a capacity on the part of all citizens to perceive and understand local/global linkages.

Unfortunately, in large measure citizenship education and "global, international, world-order, foreign affairs" education in the schools have been mutually isolated from one another.[36] In the past, this state of affairs may have been both natural and tolerable. Today it is neither. If the expanding scope and scale of global interdependence is eradicating the boundaries that once separated foreign and domestic affairs, the same forces are eroding the boundaries that once separated education about U.S. society from education about the rest of the world.

Hence, an important part of the challenge of citizenship education today is to recognize that global education and citizenship education are not mutually exclusive but instead uniquely compatible. It is possible to see examples of important elements of citizenship behavior in both global and domestic areas. Individuals can, for example, feel a sense of loyalty and belonging to the global human community as well as to a national political community; they can support international human rights as well as domestic civil rights; they face such tasks as making, judging and influencing decisions in relation to both domestic and global issues.

Notes

1. Quoted in Byron G. Massialas, *Education and the Political System* (Reading, Mass.: Addison-Wesley, 1969), p. 2.

2. John J. Patrick, "Political Socialization and Political Education in Schools" in Stanley Renshon (ed.), *Handbook of Political Socialization Research* (New York: Free Press, 1977), p. 191.

3. Ibid.

4. For the distinction between "political education," "political learning" and "political socialization" see Patrick, "Political Socialization," pp. 191-193.

5. Karen S. Dawson, "Political Education—A Challenge," *News for Teachers of Political Science* 20 (Winter 1979), p. 4.

6. Fred M. Newmann, "Building a Rationale for Civic Education," in James P. Shaver (ed.), *Building Rationales for Citizenship Education* (Washington, D.C.: National Council for the Social Studies, 1977), pp. 4-10.

7. Richard C. Remy, "The Challenge of Citizenship Education Today," paper prepared for the U.S. Office of Education, Citizen Education Staff, August 1977. The implications of this phenomenon for social studies education are considered in Richard C. Remy, "Social Studies and Citizenship Education: Elements of a Changing Relationship," *Theory and Research in Social Education* 4, no. 4 (December 1978).

8. For a discussion of competence, see Fred M. Newmann, *Education for Citizen Action* (Berkeley: McCutchan, 1975), pp. 12-40; and Robert W. White, "Motivation Reconsidered: The Concept of Competence," *Psychological Review* 66 (1959), pp. 297-333.

9. Robert C. Ziller, *The Social Self* (New York: Pergamon Press, 1973), pp. 6-8.

10. Ibid., p. 7.

11. Instructional theorists indicate that complexity in learning experiences is increasing when one or more of the following conditions are met: (1) learning experiences move from the use of concrete data to using abstract data, (2) they require learners to process an increasingly large number of variables, (3) they require learners to perform increasingly complicated tasks and/or (4) they require learners to perform an increasingly large number of tasks. Barbara J. Winston and Charlotte C. Anderson, *Skill Development in Elementary Social Studies: A New Perspective* (Boulder, Colo.: ERIC/ChESS and Social Science Education Consortium, 1977), p. 6.

12. For a discussion of such techniques, see M. Eugene Gilliom, *Practical Methods for the Social Studies* (Belmont, Cal.: Wadsworth, 1977); Lee Ehman, Howard Mehlinger and John J. Patrick, *Toward Effective Instruction in Secondary Social Studies* (Boston: Houghton Mifflin, 1974) and Richard C. Remy and Roger LaRaus, *Citizenship Decision-Making: Skill Activities and Materials, Grades 4-9* (Menlo Park, Cal.: Addison-Wesley, 1978).

13. Winston and Anderson, *Skill Development*, pp. 7-8.

14. Ibid.

15. Herbert McCloskey and Alida Brill, "Citizenship," in the 1976-77 Annual Report of the Russell Sage Foundation, p. 86.

16. Richard C. Remy, "Making, Judging and Influencing Decisions: A Focus for Citizen Education," *Social Education* 40, no. 6 (October 1976), pp. 360-66.

17. See, for example, Phillip E. Jacob and James J. Fink, "Values and Their Function in Decision-Making," *American Behavioral Scientist* 5, no. 9 (May 1962), Supplement.

18. NCSS Ad Hoc Committee on Social Studies Curriculum Guidelines, *"Revision of the NCSS Social Studies Curriculum Guidelines,"* *Social Education* 43, no. 4 (April 1979), p. 262.

19. Winston and Anderson, *Skill Development*, p. 49.

20. See, for example, Eugene Lewis, *American Politics in a Bureaucratic Age: Citizens, Constituents, Clients and Victims* (Cambridge, Mass.: Winthrop, 1977).

21. See, for example, Alan Gartner and Frank Reissman, *The Service Society and the Consumer Vanguard* (New York: Harper & Row, 1974), pp. 3-5.

22. LeAnn Meyer, "The Citizenship Education Issue: Problems and Programs," Education Commission of the States Report no. 123, February 1979, p. 20.

23. Ivor K. Davies, *The Management of Learning* (New York: McGraw-Hill, 1971); W. James Popham and Eva L. Baker, *Systematic Instruction* (Englewood Cliffs, N.J: Prentice-Hall, 1970); Ehman, Mehlinger and Patrick, *Toward Effective Instruction*, pp. 111-156 and 321-371.

24. Quoted in Robert G. Kraft, "Bike Riding and the Art of Learning," *Change*, June/July 1978, p. 41.

25. Scribner and M. Cole, "Cognitive Consequences of Formal and Informal Education," *Science*, 1973, pp. 182, 553-59. Criteria 2, 3 and 4 are based, in part, on John J. Patrick and Richard C. Remy, *Essential Learning Skills in the Education of Citizens* (Bloomington, Ind.: Agency for Instructional Television, 1977), pp. 2-4.

26. For a discussion of the natural political world of children, see Richard C. Remy, Lee F. Anderson and Richard C. Snyder, "Citizenship Education in Elementary Schools," *Theory Into Practice* 15, no. 1 (February 1976), pp. 32-33; and Lee F. Anderson, Richard C. Remy and Richard C. Snyder, "Criteria for Improving Political Education in Elementary School," *International Journal of Political Education*, no. 1 (September 1977), pp. 62-63.

27. Suzanne Wiggins Helburn, "Economics in the Curriculum," in Irving Morrissett & W. Williams Stevens (eds.), *Social Science in the Schools* (New York: Holt, Rinehart & Winston, 1971).

28. Quoted in Kraft, "Bike Riding and the Art of Learning," p. 41.

29. For an excellent discussion of citizenship, see Lee F. Anderson, *Schooling and Citizenship in a Global Age* (Bloomington, Ind.: Social Studies Development Center, Indiana University, 1979), chapter 10. See also "The Meaning of Citizenship," *Social Research* 41, no. 4 (Winter 1974); and McCloskey and Brill,

"Citizenship."

30. Anderson, *Schooling and Citizenship in a Global Age*, pp. 336-37.

31. Harold D. Lasswell, *Who Gets What, When and How* (New York: Meridian Books, World Publishing Co., 1958).

32. Robert H. Salisbury, *Key Concepts of Citizenship: Perspectives and Dilemmas* (Washington, D.C.: U.S. Department of Health, Education and Welfare, Office of Education, 1978), p. 6.

33. Salisbury, *Key Concepts of Citizenship*, p. 10. The concept of participation is much discussed in social science. See also Sidney Verba and Norman H. Nie, *Participation in America: Political Democracy and Social Equality* (New York: Harper and Row, 1972).

34. Anderson, *Schooling and Citizenship in a Global Age*, pp. 336-38.

35. Chadwick F. Alger, "Increasing Opportunities for Effective and Responsible Transnational Participation," *Mershon Center Quarterly Report* 1, no. 4 (Summer 1976), p. 2.

36. M. Eugene Gilliom and Richard C. Remy, "Needed: A New Approach to Global Education," *Social Education* 42, no. 6 (October 1978), pp. 499-503.

Bibliography

The Basic Citizenship Competencies Project has made use of extensive and diverse sources to create this annotated bibliography, which can be used as a reference for the seven citizenship competencies identified by the project. The ERIC computer information reference system was the source of extensive searches of education-related books and articles. The *Education Index* supplemented the ERIC search. Indexes of relevant social science handbooks were also examined. (A table of references to current social science theory on topics directly related to the competencies is included as part of this bibliography.) Indexes of major political science journals were also searched for articles pertaining to the competencies. Also utilized were books, articles and other materials recommended by the project's National Advisory Panel.

Books

Cleary, Robert E. *Political Education in the American Democracy.* Intext Educational Publishers, 1971. The purpose of political education in a democracy must be to develop the ability of citizens to analyze public issues in a rational way.

Entwistle, Harold. *Political Education in a Democracy.* Routledge & Kegan Paul, 1971. The "macro" approach to political education provides an unsatisfactory account of how citizens function most actively and satisfactorily in the political arena. Emphasis on citizen involvement with microinstitutions would be more appropriate.

Fox, Robert, et al., eds. *A Framework for Social Science Education.* Social Science Education Consortium, 1973. Promotes a need for curriculum revision with the students involved in data gathering, data analysis, inference testing, value judging and action designing.

Hall, Robert T., and John U. Davis. *Moral Education in Theory and Practice.* Prometheus Books, n.d. Discusses development of specific skills of decision making, the ability to envisage alternative kinds of actions, and the ability to gain some judgment of the personal and social values implicit in one's actions.

Jennings, M.K., and Richard Niemi. *The Political Character of Adolescence.* Princeton University Press, 1974. Looks at the factors that have prepared adolescents for political participation: What are their political values? What were the sources of those values?

Kurfman, Dana G., ed. *Developing Decision-Making Skills.* National Council for the Social Studies, 1977. Discussion of developing decision-making skills and its relationship to citizenship.

Newmann, Fred M. *Education for Citizen Action: Challenge for Secondary Curriculum.* McCutchan, 1975. Schools are not turning out persons competent enough to be involved in participatory democracy. Proposes an agenda for curriculum development to meet that problem.

Remy, Richard C., et al. *International Learning and International Education in a Global Age.* National Council for the Social Studies, 1975. It is important for the development of international education that teachers be aware of their own world views, alternative world views and the process of children's learning about the world.

Roelofs, H. Mark. *The Tensions of Citizenship: Private Man and Public Duty.* Rinehart, 1957. Identifies and analyzes three major values of democratic citizenship (participation, loyalty, and individualism) and examines them within the historical context in which they originated. The aim is to elucidate the social and, above all, the moral content of democratic citizenship from a historical perpective.

Shaver, James P., ed. *Building Rationales for Citizenship Education.* National Council for the Social Studies, 1977. A collection of articles on the theme of reconceptualization of and rationale building for citizenship education.

Thompson, Dennis F. *The Democratic Citizen.* Cambridge University Press, 1970. Relates a theory of democratic citizenship to studies from behavioral social science and concludes that "the findings of social science are within certain limits very useful in formulating a theory of democratic citizenship, and citizenship theory can be reconciled with and supported by these findings."

Basic Theory References

This table lists theoretical subgroups relevant to citizenship competencies as discussed in social science handbooks. Under each subgroup are handbook citations which will provide a ready reference to current theoretical statements on each topic.

Theoretical Subgroup	Citation*	Competency
Conflict		6
Bargaining theory	HPSC 1:191, 2:321	
	HPSC 8:396	
Conflict resolution	HPSC 5:321-333, 338-340,	
	342-345, 352, 354	
Dispute settlement,	HPSC 5:338	
management of	HSTR 554-557,	
	HPSC 2:326	
Measurement of conflict	HPSC 7:183-184	
of interest, theories of	HPP 4-5	
Decision Making		
Appraisal		6
alternative	HPSC 6:14-15	
base values	HPSC 6:9-10	
criteria for	HPSC 6:13-14	
goals of	HPSC 6:10-14	
participants	HPSC 6:8-9	
process of	HPSC 6:8-10	
Criteria, conflicts among	HPSC 1:349-357	6
Decision making	HPSC 1:203, 6:389	3
Decision making models	HPSC 6:390	3
Decision process	HPSC 6:1, 2, 4	3
Decision theory	HPSC 2:320, 341	3
certainty	HPSC 2:335	
and compromise	HPSC 2:326, 349	
risk	HPSC 2:320, 335	
transivity of choice	HPSC 2:326	
uncertainty	HPSC 2:320, 335-347	

*Abbreviations:

HPSC—*Handbook of Political Science Cumulative Index* (Fred I. Greenstein and Nelson W. Polsby, Addison-Wesley, 1975).
HPSO—*Handbook of Political Socialization* (Stanley A. Renshon, ed., The Free Press, 1977).
HPP—*Handbook of Political Psychology,* (Jeanne N. Knutson, ed., Jossey-Bass, 1973).
HSTR—*Handbook of Socialization Theory and Research* (David A. Goslin, ed., Rand McNally, 1973).

Theoretical Subgroup	Citation*	Competency
organizations	HPSC 4:181-182	
pressure groups	HPSC 4:176	
Politics	HPSC 7:134	
Processes, simulation of	HPP 399-406	
Small-group theory	HPSC 2:320	
Information		1
Acquisition of	HPSC 4:96	
Costs	HPSC 4:96-97, 98, 111, 121	
Gathering and cognitive theory	HSTR 338-339	
Levels of public	HPSC 4:79, 81-83, 93, 102, 156	
Processing	HSTR 579-584	
Theory	HPSC 2:332, 334	
Political Participation		
Citizen-initiated contacts	HPSC 4:10-11, 13	5
Citizenship	HPSC 3:183, 602-605, 607-608	
Leader responsiveness	HPSC 4:63-68	5
Particularized contacting	HPSC 4:21-22, 69	5
Skills	HPSO 195, 199-201, 211-212	6
Values		4
Clarification	HPSO 360	
Judgments	HPSC 1:315, 317	
Moral judgment	HPSO 339-341, 348, 349, 352	
Moral reasoning, skills of	HPSO 210-211	
Normative political inquiry	HPSC 1:314, 328	
Social structure	HSTR 618-619	

Articles

Anderson, Lee F., et al. "Criteria for Improving Political Education in Elementary School." *International Journal of Political Education* 1, no. 1 (September 1977). Proposes an approach to political education in elementary school that describes criteria to help students learn to practice citizenship. (Competency 1)

Bennett, William, and Edwin J. Delattre. "Moral Education in the Schools." *The Public Interest*, Winter 1978. Criticism of Sidney Simon's value clarification method of moral education and Kohlberg's cognitive moral development method. (4)

Bernstein, Edgar. "Citizenship and the Social Studies." *School Review* 79, no. 3 (May 1971). Says social studies should develop a sequestering of experiences and activities which will result in the development of adult capabilities for a democratic society. (1)

Beyer, Barry K., and Henry P. French. "Effective Citizenship: A Continuing Challenge." *Social Education* 29, no. 6 (October 1965). Social studies programs should develop politically competent as well as intellectually competent students. (1)

Buggey, JoAnne. "Citizenship and Community Involvement: The Primary Grades." *Social Education* 40, no. 3 (March 1976). Community involvement can be a key to successful citizenship education within the primary grades. (6)

Butts, W. Freeman. "Education for Citizenship: The Oldest, Newest Innovation in Schools." *Center for Information on America* 27, no. 8 (April 1977). Citizenship education is best achieved by allowing students to participate in choices among alternatives, through the use of acting upon their values and gaining knowledge necessary to participate in political system. School can do this by being a political system itself. (1)

Hawley, Willis. "Political Education and School Organization." *Theory Into Practice* 10, no. 5. Schools teach democracy but do not practice it. They should be organized to teach by example. (1, 3, 6)

_____. "Political Education and School Organization." *Theory Into Practice* 10, no. 5. To encourage more participatory democracy, we should change the way the schools are run and the relationship between teachers and students. (6)

Jaworski, Leon. "Leadership in Citizenship." *Today's Education* 64, no. 1 (January/February 1975). Schools need to institute and enlarge programs for youth in the fundamentals of law in a free society and in the responsibilities of leadership.

Kohlberg, Lawrence. "A Cognitive-Developmental Approach to Moral Education." *The Humanist*, December 1972. Psychological research has discovered culturally universal stages of moral development. These findings help generate a philosophy of moral education as the stimulation of moral development, rather than the teaching of fixed rules. (4)

McClelland, David. "Testing for Competence Rather Than for Intelligence" *American Psychologist,* January 1973. The author issues strong arguments against intelligence testing and suggests alternatives. (1, 2, 3, 4, 5, 6, 7).

Morgan, Edward P. "High School Learning as Political Socialization: An Experiential Approach." Paper presented to the Northeast Political Science Association, November 1977. Looks at the high school learning process as a micropolitical experience. An empirical study found that the school experience was basically hostile to the formation of democratic attitudes and behavior orientations.

Pranger, Robert J. "Experience as a Form of Political Education." Report to the 1971 meeting of the American Political Science Association, Chicago. Political education should blend abstract ideas and concrete experiences. (1)

Ravitch, Diane. "Moral Education and the Schools." *Commentary* 56, no. 3 (September 1973). All education transmits values. The school environment itself requires the continual exercise of moral choice, and is thus an excellent focus for giving children experience in evaluation and decision making.

Remy, Richard D. "High School Seniors' Attitudes Toward Their Civics and Government Instruction." *Social Education* 36, no. 6 (October 1972). Study found students wanted a change in curricula that would help them develop their abilities to analyze and evaluate political life.

_____. "Making, Judging and Influencing Political Decisions: A Focus for Citizenship Education." *Social Education* 40, no. 8 (October 1976). Classrooms must facilitate the development of decision-making capabilities in students to bridge the gap between future political choices made by students and decisions made by students in their daily lives. (1)

_____, et al. "An Experience-Based Approach to Citizenship Education in Elementary School." *Theory Into Practice* 14, no. 1 (February 1976). New programs need to make students active learners. This means they must teach competencies transferable to problems of everyday life. (1-7)

Appendix

Citizenship Competencies Checklist

			Materials					
					Criteria			
Competencies			Curriculum Materials Do They Include These?	Materials Provide for Reflection & Debriefing	Materials Are Personally Meaningful	Materials Provide for Reinforcement	Materials Provide Application	
	Yes	No						
1. *Competence in acquiring and processing information about political situations.*								
1.1 Students have the opportunity to use newspapers and magazines to obtain current information and opinions about issues and problems.								
1.2 Students have the opportunity to use books, maps, charts, graphs and other sources.								
1.3 Students have the opportunity to recognize the unique advantages and disadvantages of radio and television as sources of information about issues and problems.								
1.4 Students have the opportunity to identify and acquire information from public and private sources such as government agencies and community groups.								
1.5 Students have the opportunity to obtain information from fellow citizens by asking appropriate questions.								
1.6 Students have the opportunity to evaluate the validity and quality of information.								
1.7 Students have the opportunity to select, organize and use information collected.								

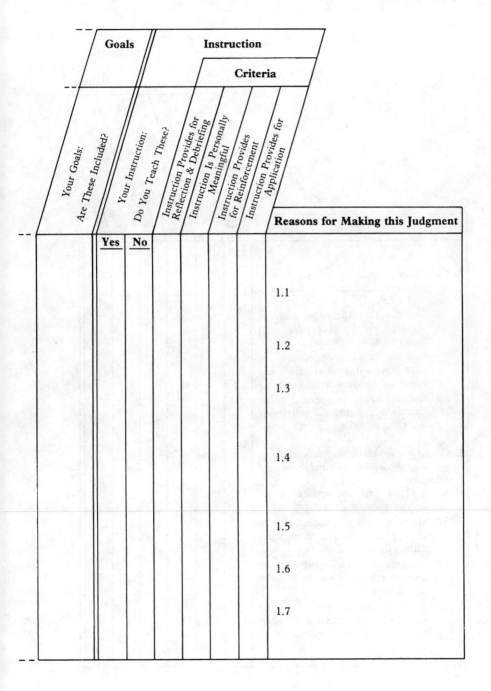

		Materials					
			Criteria				
Competencies	Curriculum Materials Do They Include These?		Materials Provide for Reflection & Debriefing	Materials Are Personally Meaningful	Materials Provide for Reinforcement	Materials Provide Application	
	Yes	No					
2. *Competence in assessing one's involvement and stake in political situations, issues, decisions and policies.*							
2.1 Students have the opportunity to identify a wide range of implications for an event or condition.							
2.2 Students have the opportunity to identify ways individual actions and beliefs can produce consequences.							
2.3 Students have the opportunity to identify their rights and obligations in a given situation.							
3. *Competence in making thoughtful decisions regarding group governance and problems of citizenship.*							
3.1 Students have the opportunity to develop realistic alternatives.							
3.2 Students have the opportunity to identify the consequences of alternatives for self and others.							
3.3 Students have the opportunity to determine goals or values involved in a decision.							
3.4 Students have the opportunity to assess the consequences of alternatives based on stated values or goals.							

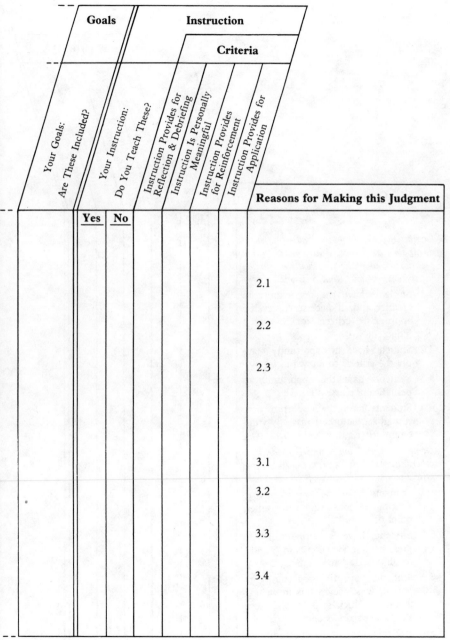

Competencies	Curriculum Materials Do They Include These?		Materials Provide for Reflection & Debriefing	Materials Are Personally Meaningful	Materials Provide for Reinforcement	Materials Provide Application
	Yes	No				
4. *Competence in developing and using standards such as justice, ethics, morality and practicality to make judgments of people, institutions, policies, and decisions.*						
4.1 Students have the opportunity to identify and, if necessary, develop appropriate criteria for making a judgment.						
4.2 Students have the opportunity to apply the criteria to known facts.						
4.3 Students have the opportunity to periodically reassess criteria.						
4.4 Students have the opportunity to recognize that others may apply different criteria to a problem.						
5. *Competence in communicating ideas to other citizens, decision makers, leaders and officials.*						
5.1 Students have the opportunity to develop reasons supporting their point of view.						
5.2 Students have the opportunity to present these viewpoints to friends, neighbors, and acquaintances.						
5.3 Students have the opportunity to present these viewpoints in writing to public officials, political leaders and to newspapers and magazines.						
5.4 Students have the opportunity to present these viewpoints at public meetings such as committees, school board meetings, city government sessions, etc.						

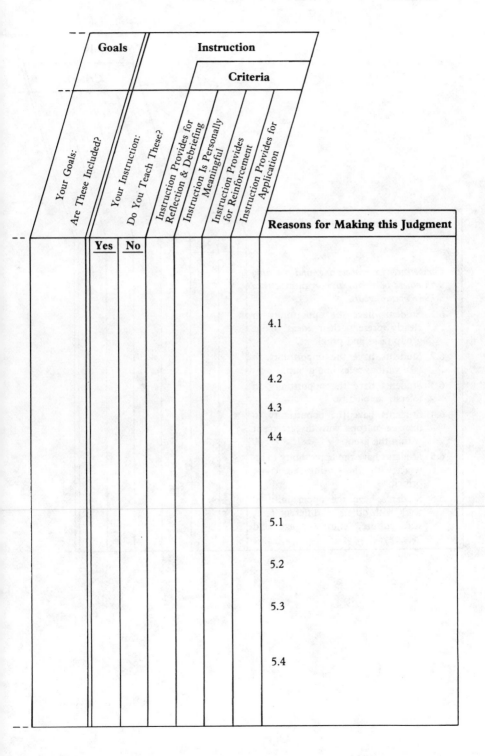

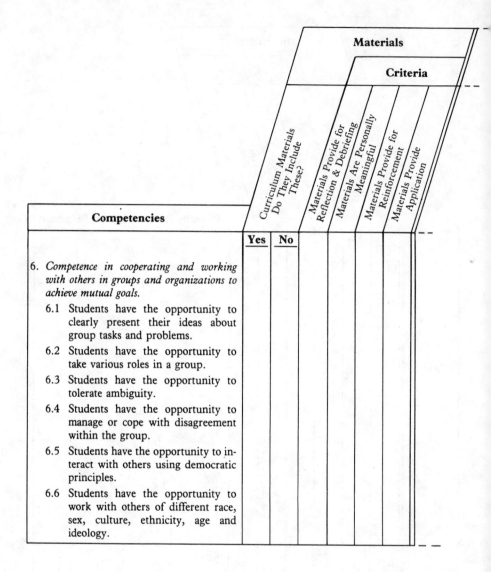

Competencies	Curriculum Materials Do They Include These?		Materials Provide for Reflection & Debriefing	Materials Are Personally Meaningful	Materials Provide for Reinforcement	Materials Provide Application
	Yes	No				
6. *Competence in cooperating and working with others in groups and organizations to achieve mutual goals.*						
6.1 Students have the opportunity to clearly present their ideas about group tasks and problems.						
6.2 Students have the opportunity to take various roles in a group.						
6.3 Students have the opportunity to tolerate ambiguity.						
6.4 Students have the opportunity to manage or cope with disagreement within the group.						
6.5 Students have the opportunity to interact with others using democratic principles.						
6.6 Students have the opportunity to work with others of different race, sex, culture, ethnicity, age and ideology.						

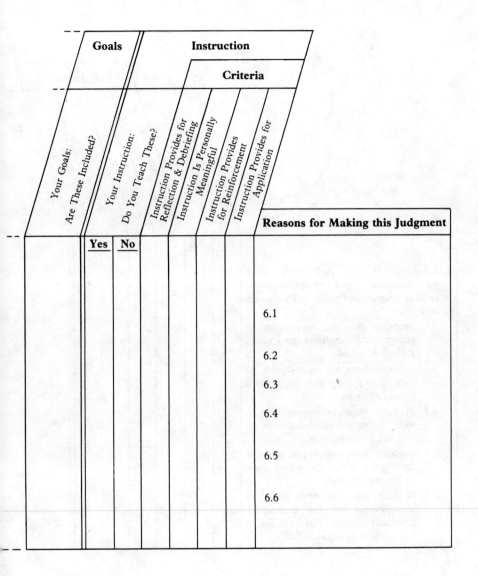

Goals		Instruction						Reasons for Making this Judgment
				Criteria				
Your Goals: Are These Included?		Your Instruction: Do You Teach These?	Instruction Provides for Reflection & Debriefing	Instruction Is Personally Meaningful	Instruction Provides for Reinforcement	Instruction Provides for Application		
Yes	No							
								6.1
								6.2
								6.3
								6.4
								6.5
								6.6

Competencies	Curriculum Materials Do They Include These?		Materials Provide for Reflection & Debriefing	Materials Are Personally Meaningful	Materials Provide for Reinforcement	Materials Provide Application
	Yes	No				
7. Competence in working with bureaucratically organized institutions in order to promote and protect one's interests and values.						
7.1 Students have the opportunity to recognize their interests and goals in a given situation.						
7.2 Students have the opportunity to identify an appropriate strategy for a given situation.						
7.3 Students have the opportunity to work through organized groups to support their interests.						
7.4 Students have the opportunity to use legal remedies to protect their rights and interests.						
7.5 Students have the opportunity to identify and use the established grievance procedures within a bureaucracy or organization.						

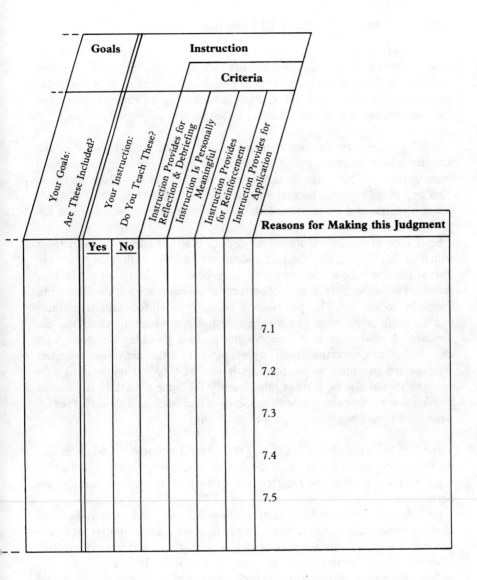

Instructions for Numerical Scoring

Step 1: Indicating Whether Capacities Are Present or Absent. You should first indicate whether a capacity is included or not included by placing an "X" in either the "Yes" or "No" subcolumn. If you are assessing curriculum materials, these subcolumns are numbers 2 and 3; if you are assessing instructional programs, these subcolumns are numbers 9 and 10. See sample on pages 94-95.

Step 2: Indicating the Extent of Professional Satisfaction. After you have decided whether opportunities are provided to learn each of the capacities and finished marking the "Yes/No" subcolumns, you are ready to proceed to the next task. This step is more precise because you are asked to indicate the extent to which you as a professional are satisfied with the quality of the particular learning opportunities provided.

Score each of four subcolumns provided for evaluating learning experiences with a "1" or "0." If, for example, students are provided with opportunities to discuss and think about what they have done, place a "1" in the subcolumn for reflection and debriefing. If such opportunities are not provided, the subcolumn should be coded "0." This procedure is followed for all four criteria columns and the result is totaled to indicate the extent of your satisfaction with that experience. A total score of 4 indicates the greatest possible satisfaction with capacity-building opportunities and a score of 0 the least. When no opportunities are provided and the "No" subcolumn is marked "X," all four criteria subcolumns should also be marked "0." Exactly the same procedure is followed whether you are assessing curriculum materials (subcolumns 2 through 7) or instructional programs (subcolumns 9 through 14).

Step 3: Scoring the Checklist. Totaling the scores is a simple procedure requiring three computations. First, total the four subcolumns in the checklist that indicate extent of professional satisfaction with the capacity-building learning opportunities.

For example, the completed sample shows that the first capacity-building learning opportunity (1.1) is considered not to provide opportunities for reflection but that is is personally meaningful, is reinforcing, and actively involves students. Thus, the total score for this capacity is 3. The second capacity-building learning opportunity (1.2) is both meaningful to students and reinforced consistently. The total score for this capacity is 2.

After the criteria subcolumns are totaled to determine professional satisfaction with each capacity, these scores are added together to obtain a raw score for the entire competency. In our sample, the raw score for Competency 1 is 10. In order for the raw score to be meaningful, it is necessary to determine what percentage of the total possible score it represents. To do this, divide the raw score by the total possible score. For the Competency 1 example, this figure is $(10 \div 28 =)$ .36, or 36 percent.

Step 4: Using the Individual Computation Sheet: The Individual Computation Sheet can be used to summarize information about all of the competencies and capacities. The boxes across the top of the computation sheet refer to individual competency scores. (The figure for Competency 1 is 36 percent in the example.) Transfer the total scores for each competency from the checklist to the boxes.

Step 5: Adjusting the Competency Scores. The chart at the bottom of the computation sheet requires that the raw score for each competency be entered in the first column. After entering the raw score, multiply it by an adjustment factor so that the scores for each competency have equal weight. For example, seven capacities are necessary to demonstrate competence in acquiring information, three to demonstrate competency in assessing involvement, four in making decisions, four in making judgments, four in communicating, six in cooperating, and five in promoting interests. Multiply the raw score for each competency by the appropriate adjustment factor and enter that figure into the adjusted score column. The total of all adjusted scores is the total adjusted competency score.

Step 6: Converting the total adjusted competency score to a percentage. Divide the total adjusted competency score by the maximum possible score (84). (The adjustment factors and the maximum possible score are entered on the Individual Computation Sheet for your convenience.)

Sample of Numerical Scoring for Checklist

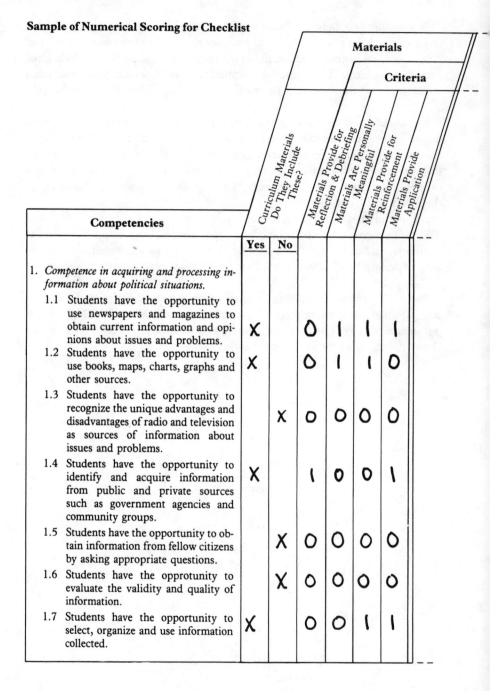

Competencies	Curriculum Materials Do They Include These? (Yes)	(No)	Materials Provide for Reflection & Debriefing	Materials Are Personally Meaningful	Materials Provide for Reinforcement	Materials Provide Application
1. Competence in acquiring and processing information about political situations.						
1.1 Students have the opportunity to use newspapers and magazines to obtain current information and opinions about issues and problems.	X		O	I	I	I
1.2 Students have the opportunity to use books, maps, charts, graphs and other sources.	X		O	I	I	O
1.3 Students have the opportunity to recognize the unique advantages and disadvantages of radio and television as sources of information about issues and problems.		X	O	O	O	O
1.4 Students have the opportunity to identify and acquire information from public and private sources such as government agencies and community groups.	X		I	O	O	I
1.5 Students have the opportunity to obtain information from fellow citizens by asking appropriate questions.		X	O	O	O	O
1.6 Students have the opprotunity to evaluate the validity and quality of information.		X	O	O	O	O
1.7 Students have the opportunity to select, organize and use information collected.	X		O	O	I	I

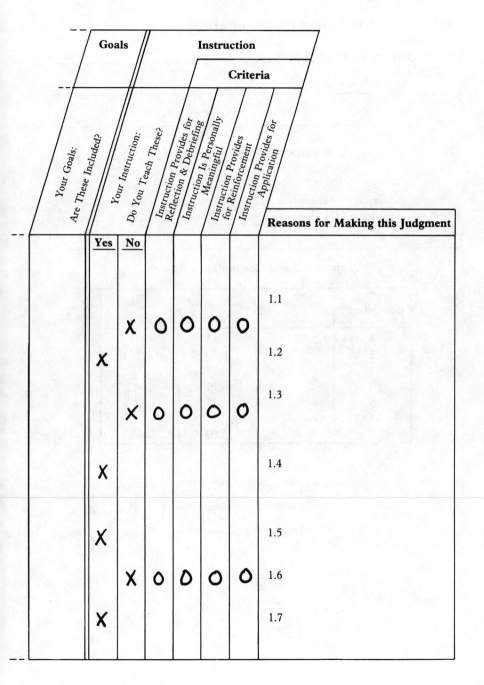

Your Goals: Are These Included?	Your Instruction: Do You Teach These?		Instruction Provides for Reflection & Debriefing	Instruction Is Personally Meaningful	Instruction Provides for Reinforcement	Instruction Provides for Application	Reasons for Making this Judgment
	Yes	No					
		X	O	O	O	O	1.1
	X						1.2
		X	O	O	O	O	1.3
	X						1.4
	X						1.5
		X	O	O	O	O	1.6
	X						1.7

Individual Computation Sheet

Unit or Materials Analyzed: _____

_____

School: _____

Individual Competency Scores

1 Acquiring Information	2 Assessing Involvement	3 Making Decisions	4 Making Judgments	5 Communi- cating	6 Coop- erating	7 Promoting Interests

Adjusted Total Competency Score

Competency	Raw Score	X Adjustment Factor	= Adjusted Score
1		.43	
2		1.00	
3		.75	
4		.75	
5		.75	
6		.50	
7		.60	

Total adjusted competency score _____

÷ Maximum possible score   84

=   Total competency score   _____ %

Checklist for Parents

When we think of citizenship education, we are likely to think of the schools. Yet the task of citizenship education today is not confined to elementary and high schools. There are many agents or sources of learning in the process of citizen development. One of the most important of these is the family. The very nature of childhood makes the family environment a key influence in the process of citizen development. The family has direct access to the developing citizen. During the very early years this approaches a monopoly. In addition, intense emotional and personal ties are usually forged among members of the same family. Further, the almost total dependence of children on their parents for basic needs gives them little opportunity to resist parents' pressure to conform.

The family contributes to the process of citizen development in several ways. Parents pass on explicitly political orientations to their children through discussion, by modeling behavior, and by other means. In addition, the family shapes the basic personality, social outlook and self-concept of the maturing child—orientations very relevant to the development of citizen competence. Finally, the family influences the young child's exposure to other agents of citizen development. Friends, schools, recreational groups and the like are largely determined by the family.

The following checklist can be used to help sensitize parents to their role in the citizenship education process. The checklist is organized around the seven basic competencies described in the handbook.

Guiding Questions	Learning Opportunities Provided		
	Many	Some	None
Competency 1: Acquiring and Using Information			
—Do I help my children find information from many sources?			
—Do I help them choose information that is useful in solving problems?			
—Do I encourage them to organize information in a way that helps them to achieve their goals?			
Competency 2: Assessing Involvement			
—Do I help my children identify why a situation may be important to them?			

	Learning Opportunities Provided		
Guiding Questions	Many	Some	None
—Do I help them to see how their actions may affect others?			
—Do I help them to see how their failure to act may affect themselves and others?			
Competency 3: Making Decisions			
—Do I help my children consider many alternatives when they make decisions?			
—Do I ask them to consider the results of different decisions?			
—Do I encourage them to participate in family decisions?			
Competency 4: Making Judgments			
—Do I help my children develop standards for making political judgments?			
—Do I encourage them to use their guidelines consistently?			
—Do I respect and listen to their judgments?			
Competency 5: Communicating			
—Do I help my children prepare good arguments supporting their points of view?			
—Do I listen to their arguments and consider them when making family decisions?			
—Do I encourage them to write to public officials or share their opinions orally at school?			
Competency 6: Cooperating With Others			
—Do I work with my children in achieving family goals?			

	Learning Opportunities Provided		
Guiding Questions	Many	Some	None
—Do I encourage them to participate in many groups, both as leaders and as followers?			
—Do I encourage them to work cooperatively with people of both sexes and many different races, cultures, and ages?			
Competency 7: Promoting Interests			
—Do I help them to learn about large institutions?			
—Do I help them identify ways of protecting their rights and interests?			

ASCD Publications, Spring 1980

Yearbooks

Considered Action for Curriculum Improvement (610-80186) $9.75

Education for an Open Society (610-74012) $8.00

Education for Peace: Focus on Mankind (610-17946) $7.50

Evaluation as Feedback and Guide (610-17700) $6.50

Feeling, Valuing, and the Art of Growing: Insights into the Affective (610-77104) $9.75

Freedom, Bureaucracy, & Schooling (610-17508) $6.50

Improving the Human Condition: A Curricular Response to Critical Realities (610-78132) $9.75

Learning and Mental Health in the School (610-17674) $5.00

Life Skills in School and Society (610-17786) $5.50

Lifelong Learning—A Human Agenda (610-79160) $9.75

A New Look at Progressive Education (610-17812) $8.00

Perspectives on Curriculum Development 1776-1976   (610-76078) $9.50

Schools in Search of Meaning (610-75044) $8.50

Perceiving, Behaving, Becoming: A New Focus for Education   (610-17278) $5.00

To Nurture Humaneness: Commitment for the '70's   (610-17810) $6.00

Books and Booklets

About Learning Materials   (611-78134) $4.50

Action Learning: Student Community Service Projects   (611-74018) $2.50

Adventuring, Mastering, Associating: New Strategies for Teaching Children (611-76080) $5.00

Beyond Jencks: The Myth of Equal Schooling (611-17928) $2.00

Bilingual Education for Latinos (611-78142) $6.75

The Changing Curriculum: Mathematics (611-17724) $2.00

Classroom-Relevant Research in the Language Arts   (611-78140) $7.50

Clinical Supervision—A State of the Art Review (611-80194) $3.75

Criteria for Theories of Instruction (611-17756) $2.00

Curricular Concerns in a Revolutionary Era (611-17852) $6.00

Curriculum Leaders: Improving Their Influence (611-76084) $4.00

Curriculum Theory   (611-77112) $7.00

Degrading the Grading Myths: A Primer of Alternatives to Grades and Marks (611-76082) $6.00

Differentiated Staffing   (611-17924) $3.50

Discipline for Today's Children and Youth (611-17314) $1.50

Educational Accountability: Beyond Behavioral Objectives   (611-17856) $2.50

Elementary School Mathematics: A Guide to Current Research   (611-75056) $5.00

Elementary School Science: A Guide to Current Research   (611-17726) $2.25

Eliminating Ethnic Bias in Instructional Materials: Comment and Bibliography (611-74020) $3.25

Emerging Moral Dimensions in Society: Implications for Schooling (611-75052) $3.75

Ethnic Modification of the Curriculum (611-17832) $1.00

Global Studies: Problems and Promises for Elementary Teachers   (611-76086) $4.50

Handbook of Basic Citizenship Competencies (611-80196) $4.75

Humanistic Education: Objectives and Assessment   (611-78136) $4.75

The Humanities and the Curriculum (611-17708) $2.00

Impact of Decentralization on Curriculum: Selected Viewpoints   (611-75050) $3.75

Improving Educational Assessment & An Inventory of Measures of Affective Behavior   (611-17804) $4.50

International Dimension of Education (611-17816) $2.25

Interpreting Language Arts Research for the Teacher   (611-17846) $4.00

Learning More About Learning (611-17310) $2.00

Linguistics and the Classroom Teacher (611-17720) $2.75

A Man for Tomorrow's World (611-17838) $2.25

Middle School in the Making (611-74024) $5.00

The Middle School We Need (611-75060) $2.50

Moving Toward Self-Directed Learning (611-79166) $4.75

Multicultural Education: Commitments, Issues, and Applications   (611-77108) $7.00

Needs Assessment: A Focus for Curriculum Development   (611-75048) $4.00

Observational Methods in the Classroom (611-17948) $3.50

Open Education: Critique and Assessment (611-75054) $4.75

Partners: Parents and Schools (611-79168) $4.75

Professional Supervision for Professional Teachers   (611-75046) $4.50

Removing Barriers to Humaneness in the High School   (611-17848) $2.50

Reschooling Society: A Conceptual Model (611-17950) $2.00

The School of the Future—NOW (611-17920) $3.75

Schools Become Accountable: A PACT Approach   (611-74016) $3.50

The School's Role as Moral Authority (611-77110) $4.50

Selecting Learning Experiences: Linking Theory and Practice   (611-78138) $4.75

Social Studies for the Evolving Individual (611-17952) $3.00

Staff Development: Staff Liberation (611-77106) $6.50

Supervision: Emerging Profession (611-17796) $5.00

Supervision in a New Key   (611-17926) $2.50

Supervision: Perspectives and Propositions (611-17732) $2.00

What Are the Sources of the Curriculum? (611-17522) $1.50

Vitalizing the High School   (611-74026) $3.50

Developmental Characteristics of Children and Youth (wall chart)   (611-75058) $2.00

Discounts on quantity orders of same title to single address: 10-49 copies, 10%; 50 or more copies, 15%. Make checks or money orders payable to ASCD. Orders totaling $10.00 or less must be prepaid. Orders from institutions and businesses must be on official purchase order form. Shipping and handling charges will be added to billed purchase orders. *Please be sure to list the stock number of each publication, shown in parentheses.*

Subscription to *Educational Leadership*—$15.00 a year. ASCD Membership dues: Regular (subscription [$15] and yearbook)—$29.00 a year; Comprehensive (includes subscription [$15] and yearbook plus other books and booklets distributed during period of membership)—$39.00 a year.

Order from:

Association for Supervision and Curriculum Development
225 North Washington Street
Alexandria, Virginia 22314